FINDING
A
HIGHER
LOVE

ELIZABETH CLARE PROPHET

FINDING
A
HIGHER
LOVE

A Spiritual Guide to
LOVE, SEX & RELATIONSHIPS

SUMMIT UNIVERSITY PRESS®

Gardiner, Montana

FINDING A HIGHER LOVE
A Spiritual Guide to Love, Sex and Relationships
by Elizabeth Clare Prophet
Copyright © 2015 Summit Publications, Inc.
All rights reserved.

For information, contact Summit University Press,
63 Summit Way, Gardiner, MT 59030 USA
Tel: 1-800-245-5445 or 406-848-9500
www.SummitUniversityPress.com

Library of Congress Control Number: 2015931633
ISBN: 978-1-60988-262-4 (softbound)
ISBN: 978-1-60988-263-1 (eBook)

SUMMIT UNIVERSITY ♨ PRESS®

Summit University Press and ♨ are trademarks registered in the U.S. Patent and Trademark Office and in other countries. All rights reserved

Cover photo: © Sardorrr | Dreamstime.com - Two Hands Reaching For Each Other Photo

Printed in the United States of America
19 18 17 16 15   1 2 3 4 5

Disclaimer: No guarantee is made by Summit University Press that the spiritual practices described in this book will yield successful results for anyone at any time. The practice and proof of the science of being rests with the individual.

CONTENTS

LIST OF ILLUSTRATIONS

NOTE TO THE READER

For many years Elizabeth Clare Prophet conducted seminars throughout the world on the subject of twin flames, soul mates, and karmic relationships. Some believe her to be the foremost expert in this field. *Finding a Higher Love: A Spiritual Guide to Love, Sex and Relationships* is a compilation of her practical and uplifting teachings. Also included are questions and answers from her many public seminars.

We express our gratitude to all those who contributed to this labor of love.

SUMMIT UNIVERSITY PRESS

FOREWORD

Shakespeare wrote that all the world is a stage where people have their exits and entrances and each person in his time plays many parts.

Imagine Shakespeare's world as a classroom for our souls. In Shakespeare's plays and in our real lives, it is relationships—both with ourselves and with others—that provide many of the lessons we need to learn in order to reach a higher love.

In our sojourn on earth, we have entered and exited the stage of life again and again, and we have played many parts. We have journeyed through the ages, encountering other souls and engaging in relationships, seeking love. Sometimes we stay together for a lifetime; other times we share brief interchanges. We remain single, we marry, we have children, sometimes we separate or get divorced. We lose love and find love in unexpected ways. By the offering of profound love and forgiveness, some of our greatest challenges are transformed, and then our souls feel free. Throughout this journey, we continue our search.

As we navigate relationships, we strive for understanding, but often the deeper meaning of our encounters eludes us. Yet seeing from a different viewpoint, we can begin to unveil the inner mysteries of love, sex, and relationships. Unlike other books, this one looks at these topics from the perspective of the soul. It presents the understanding that regardless of our past we can change the way we view our life and our relationships forever. And it is the soul that is the missing link.

Our relationships, from the most joyful to the most painful, are an integral part of our soul's path to wholeness. Our yearning for this wholeness stems from a deep memory of union with the one soul who was created with us in the beginning—our twin flame. Having become separated, we are now on a path to reunion with that beloved one. And the key to becoming one with our twin flame is to first become one with the most real part of ourself, our Higher Self.

In *Finding a Higher Love: A Spiritual Guide to Love, Sex and Relationships,* Elizabeth Clare Prophet offers a compassionate understanding that can guide your path homeward and quicken your steps to the heart of your true love.

PART ONE

TWIN FLAMES
and
SOUL MATES

*Your soul's inner recognition
of being one half of the whole
goads her toward wholeness,
toward finding her other half.*

CHAPTER 1

THE SOUL'S SEARCH *for* DIVINE LOVE

*D*eep within our soul there is a yearning for our divine counterpart. For we have a memory from long ago of union with the one soul who is our other half, our twin flame. We were one with that soul in the beginning, when we were created, but we became separated. And then our search began.

For me this yearning was a search for my teacher and in him I found my twin flame. This was a great and profound experience—to know my twin flame as my teacher and to recognize in his eyes what I had been searching for all of my life. From early childhood I had been searching for those eyes, and I had looked into a thousand faces, a thousand, ten thousand times.

Many of us search for love, for a permanent, lasting love. We may go from relationship to relationship, seeking those eyes midst a sea of people. We yearn to be known for our souls, to be known for our true essence.

One of the most tender and moving experiences of my life happened after I had known my twin flame for many years. One day I was walking down the street with him and he said, "Elizabeth, I love you. I love your soul." The expression on his face—his love, his presence—showed a genuine caring and faithfulness to my soul. It was the tenderness of God that I felt through his heart.

I remember how I wept because for the first time in my life I realized that someone who had the capacity to know my soul actually loved my soul, just the way it was. After hearing his words, it took me about a day to regain my composure; I was so profoundly touched that someone deeply loved my inner being.

If someone truly loves you for who you are, you know that you can make it. You know that you can go on. You know that you can become the fullness of your true self. And this is the nature of friendship with God and close relationships between souls who are striving.

THE STORY *of* YOUR SOUL

You and your twin flame share the same blueprint of identity, like the design of a snowflake, unique in all of cosmos. Your soul's inner recognition of being one half of the whole goads her* toward wholeness, toward finding her other half. This goad becomes a tremendous longing for your beloved, your twin flame. Such is the yearning for the bliss of reunion—a bliss beyond any earthly experience. It is a profound union at the level of God. And your soul remembers.

From the beginning your soul has been a continuum in God. Within her resides a tremendous amount of knowledge and an awareness so vast that it is beyond description. As pure souls suspended in Spirit, you and your twin flame share this unique awareness and memory.

Lifetime after lifetime your soul grows and develops a distinct soul-identity. She may develop a talent for art, music, or other specific gifts. Each soul is supremely individual. Your soul has full conscious

---

*The soul of man and woman is feminine in relation to the masculine, or spirit, portion of being. The soul is therefore often referred to as "she" or "her."

awareness of who she is and what she has accomplished in past lives before coming into a new life. Most importantly, she knows what she needs to accomplish in her next life to make the greatest possible spiritual progress.

For before birth, your soul is shown her mission for that life. It may involve righting the wrongs that she has done to others by serving them in love and extending forgiveness. It may involve pursuing a particular profession or bringing compassion into the world. Whatever it is, that mission is specific for each soul, and each soul can choose whether or not to fulfill it.

As the soul is striving to fulfill her mission, she also has a sense of her twin flame and other souls, particularly those whom she must meet in order to resolve the past. For the soul is in touch with all life. She feels the joy of the unity of life and the pain of separation. Thus she is wise but also fragile. This fragility is in part because she is not yet permanent. She is the nonpermanent potential of being that will become permanent when she is fused to her Real Self, her Higher Self. This Higher Self is each one's own inner teacher and voice of conscience. It is one's guardian, dearest friend, and advocate before God.

The soul, who would bond with her Higher Self, is sensitive and intuitive. She is vulnerable, impressionable, and innocent. The soul mirrors whatever she puts her attention on. She is often colored by her surroundings and easily led astray. She is wounded by mental and emotional toxins and by physical or verbal abuse. These experiences, many involving relationships, create part of her karma and her psychology.

Therefore, on the journey back to her spiritual home, our soul needs our comfort and consolation, our soothing words. She needs to know that we will protect her from harm. We can lovingly care for our soul as we would care for our children, or we can neglect her. Part of the care for our soul is to immerse her in beauty and the light of God.

THE SOUL'S SPIRITUAL PATH

In the deep knowledge of our soul, we remember our beginning. We remember that with our twin flame we were originally all light and dwelled in the planes of Spirit. But we descended into the material universe and got separated from each other, and we journeyed far away from our spiritual home.

What does it mean to be on a path back to our ultimate home—a spiritual path? The word *spirit* comes from the Latin *spiritus,* meaning "breath," "breath of a god," or "inspiration." Spirituality is to the soul what the breath of life is to a newborn child. It infuses us with new life and vigor. It empowers us to love and nourish ourself and others.

Spirituality is being able to sustain a working relationship with God—with the presence of God within you, the God Presence, or I AM Presence. It is the all-loving one, sometimes called the Father-Mother God.

But it doesn't matter what you call that God—the Divine Self, the Inner Light, the Dharmakaya, Brahman, Adonai. It is possible for each of us to get in touch, and stay in touch, with the universal power of God through our heart. For God has placed within our heart a spark of divine love. It is the abiding place of God's love for our soul and our soul's love for God.

Part of being able to make this connection is our ability to engage our will in striving for our God. We came with this will, called free will, which is God's gift to us through which we can choose to walk a spiritual path and also to accomplish our purpose in life. So while each of us has a unique divine plan, it is not guaranteed. Rather, we need to exercise our free will in order to fulfill our individual divine plan, and we must do this even in the midst of distractions, impediments, and all manner of negative influences.

People sometimes think in terms of predestination and destiny. But in reality we determine the outcome of our fate every day by the freewill choices of what we do with our circumstances. And *circum-stances* is another word for karma.

KARMA

Karma is a manifestation of God's unconditional love, for it is precisely because God loves us that he allows our karma to return to us. It impels us to learn to do unto others as we would have them do unto us, and this helps our soul develop. Thus the law of karma is the law of love. It teaches us compassion as well as humility, empathy, mercy, and sensitivity to life. It brings remorse and reconciliation. It teaches us to love as no other process can or does.

Karma is a Sanskrit word meaning "act," "action," "work," or "deed." Hinduism and Buddhism teach that the law of karma is the universal law of cause and effect, which affects everyone. In other words, whatever we have done will come full circle to our doorstep, whether it is positive or negative. This is reflected in the saying "What goes around comes around."

Therefore the daily encounters of man and woman on the streets of life are, in reality, the unwinding of the cycles of karma, of positive and negative forces come full circle for resolution. Strewn along the path that we have walked for tens of thousands of years, we find all of our sowings—all the seeds we have carelessly dropped that have come to naught or borne bad fruit and all that we have meticulously planted that have grown and flourished as the bounty of our soul's striving.

Positive karma can manifest as anything from a supportive circle of family and friends to genius, aptitudes, and talents. Our positive karma and momentums can even launch us like a rocket ship on the pathway of our soul's mission with our twin flame. Negative karma can manifest as anything from a minor inconvenience to a major event in our life. It can show up as disease, accidents, or difficult relationships.

Karma is a burden of substance that is like a cloud. One day the clouds cover the sun and the next day the sky is crystal clear. We can be convinced that a relationship is all right one day, and the next day the relationship is problematical, as if the whole atmosphere is full of darkness and we can't even tell that there is a sun in the sky. That's because it is a day of karma balancing.

When this karma descends, we have a choice. We can either follow the tendency of our karma and our past, or we can change it. Experiencing the return of negative karma is sometimes painful, but pain can be a teacher and a purifier.

Balancing karma is a joyous path because we are paying our karmic debts step-by-step and eventually we will be absolved of our karma fully and finally. When we get on the right side of our karma, it will work to our benefit. It will open the door for a higher love and for blessings to continually multiply and increase.

LIFETIMES *of* LOVE

On our soul's journey, the path of balancing karma implies reincarnation. Karma necessitates rebirth because we are not able to reap all the effects of our karma or learn all our lessons in a single lifetime. Instead, we come back multiple times to experience the return of, or compensation for, all that we have done. These lifetimes stretch across the ages because we need to reembody at the same time as others with whom we have both positive and negative karma.

Our soul will return lifetime after lifetime, putting on garments of flesh, like an overcoat she has put on many times before. And one day she will take off that garment for the last time because she will not need to embody anymore.

In each lifetime, we will encounter many relationships based on both positive karma and karmic situations that need to be balanced. While balancing karma in relationships will be different for each person, our souls become more whole in the process. So through these relationships we continue our upward trek and our quest for a higher love. The search begins afresh in each lifetime when souls come "trailing clouds of glory," as Wordsworth wrote in his "Ode: Intimations of Immortality."

> Our birth is but a sleep and a forgetting;
> The Soul that rises with us, our life's Star,
> Hath had elsewhere its setting,
> And cometh from afar:
> Not in entire forgetfulness,
> And not in utter nakedness,
> But trailing clouds of glory do we come
> From God, who is our home.
>
> —WILLIAM WORDSWORTH

CHAPTER 2

TWIN FLAMES

The soul recognition of one's twin flame may happen gradually, like the morning light that gently appears. Or it may be like a lightning strike that in one swift flash illumines your life and changes it forever. Sometimes one person knows, while the other has to be graciously reminded, as in the following true story, which reflects the inner recognition that can be experienced by twin flames.

The time is the eighteenth century and the place is Germany. This is the story of the grandfather of Felix Mendelssohn, the prolific German composer. Felix's grandfather's name was Moses Mendelssohn. Moses was a renowned Jewish philosopher. He strongly believed and argued on behalf of the existence of God and the soul's immortality. One of his admirers described him as "a man of keen insight... frank and openhearted." Moses Mendelssohn was far from being a handsome man. Along with a rather short stature, he also possessed a grotesque humpback.

One day, he visited a Hamburg merchant who had a lovely daughter named Frumtje. Moses fell hopelessly in

*love with this young woman. But alas, Frumtje was re-
pulsed by his misshapen appearance. Finally, the time
came for farewells at the merchant's home. He bade the
merchant farewell and then paused as he approached the
door. Moses gathered his courage and then began to climb
the stairs to Frumtje's room to bid her farewell. He
knocked gently on the wooden door and after a few moments the door opened. Frumtje was a vision of heavenly
beauty—but her beauty caused him such deep sadness by
her refusal to even look up at him. Her gaze was fixed on
the floor. They took chairs not far from one another.*

*After several attempts at conversation, none of which
were successful, Moses shyly questioned, "Do you believe
marriages are made in heaven?" There was a long pause.
"Yes," she answered, still looking away from Moses and
staring at the floor. Another long pause ensued. And then
Frumtje quietly asked, "And do you?" Moses replied:
"Yes, I do."*

*Then Moses said, "You see, in heaven at the birth of
each boy, the Lord announces, 'This boy will marry that
particular girl.' And when I was born, my future bride was
pointed out to me, and then the Lord said, 'But, your wife
will be humpbacked.' Right then and there I called out, 'O
Lord, a humpbacked woman would be a tragedy. Please,
Lord, give me the hump and let her be beautiful.'"*

*A hush settled over the room. Frumtje slowly raised
her head and looked up into his eyes. She was stirred by
some deep memory. She reached out and gave Moses her
hand, and it was not long afterward that Frumtje became
Moses Mendelssohn's devoted wife.*[1]

At a soul level we remember our twin flame, our origin, and
our own divine nature. We remember that once we were all light in

a Spirit cosmos and that in truth we are far more than what we experience in our present condition.

If we envision the magnificent spiritual energy of God, we can see this as the greatest concentration of energy in our cosmos—a brilliant white-fire core, with thousands, tens of thousands, millions of galaxies revolving around this sun center. From out of this scintillating core, innumerable spheres of light come forth, each one a single white-fire body, a fiery ovoid of Spirit. (See Plate 1*a*.)

Each white-fire sphere of light moves with a whirling action and produces a polarity, a tai chi, which becomes the masculine and feminine aspects of God. (See Plate 1*b*.) And then, just as a cell divides through fission, the polarity separates. There are now two identical spheres of light, which become the masculine and feminine aspects of God's wholeness—two flames, twin flames. The two twin flames are each stamped with the same divine blueprint. This is their God-identity, their own God Presence, which is a frequency and an electronic pattern unique to these two and not duplicated anywhere in cosmos. It is the Presence of God individualized for each one. (See Plate 2*a*.)

From each God Presence a ray descends; it is the soul that is the counterpart of the Spirit sphere. For each pair of twin souls, one soul represents the feminine polarity; the other, the masculine. (See Plate 2*b*.)

As twin souls, our original destiny was to come forth from Spirit and, through a series of masculine and feminine lifetimes, to expand the gifts of our union in the matter cosmos. At this level of harmony, we were always one, never separated. However, we made karma and found ourselves farther and farther from each other. By and by, we developed a tremendous longing in our souls, a longing for God—the God we knew in the beginning, who created us—and a longing for the divine counterpart.

THE MASCULINE-FEMININE BALANCE

As you continue to journey through your lifetimes on earth, you and your twin flame assume all types of relationships with one another. You may be husband and wife, father and daughter, mother and son, sister and brother, friend, coworker, or another relationship. Every relationship will occur somewhere, sometime, in some lifetime.

Still needing to develop the divine qualities of the Father-Mother God, you and your twin flame experience both masculine and feminine lifetimes. But even through these lifetimes, each one of you essentially carries one half of the whole, one particular half of the polarity. Each one of you will still be slightly more male and the other more female.

If you are a man in this lifetime, you are about 60 percent masculine, 40 percent feminine; if you are a woman, you are about 60 percent feminine and 40 percent masculine. This imbalance contributes to the desire for oneness with one's counterpart.

One day when your soul completely reunites with God, you will be expressing equally the balance of masculine and feminine attributes. You will be androgynous, with the masculine-feminine balance closer to fifty-fifty. And when you reunite with your twin flame, together you will be the divine whole in perfect balance, and yet the polarity will still exist.

This is the saga of our evolution. When we awaken to the soul memory of our creation, suddenly it is not merely the present lifetime and circumstances that define us. Rather, we can trace our lives back through many lifetimes, and in these we see the weavings of both positive and negative karma that have taken us through the labyrinth of myriad levels of experience, in many ages and times past.

When we have such glimpses of our soul's experience, life takes on new meaning. We are not only on a search for a good match in this life, but we are on a search for our twin flame and for the wholeness of our original God-identity.

As we briefly capture that memory, we realize the original one-ness of our twin flames in God. A delicate note is struck, and we sense the leaping of those flames in God before we ever took form. Our hearts are again enflamed with a yearning for that reunion, and we seek in earnest the other half of our divine whole.

THE QUEST

As the search is renewed in this life, we may have many ques-tions. Where is my twin flame? Is he or she my age? Is he or she like me or different? Our twin flame may or may not be in embodiment upon earth but may be in the heaven, or etheric, world. We may be the half who is still on earth working through our karma.

Those of us who have strong ties to God and to heaven, who are very devout, often have a twin flame in heaven. We may be drawn to a spiritual or monastic life. Some of us may take vows to be wed to God. For we feel a certain internal wholeness that is our sense of union with a soul who is beyond this world, though we may not know this consciously.

If our twin flame is at the same level on the spiritual path and is in embodiment, we may long for and seek that one. On the other hand, if our twin flame is not on a spiritual path and has more worldly ties, we may experience a great dichotomy. We may love the spiritual path, but at the same time we may feel compelled to per-petually seek relationships in this world. Somewhere in all of these temporal pulls is our other half, whom we feel dedicated to rescue and to raise up. We may go from one relationship to the next, searching for that one whom we know exists somewhere, somehow. In the process, we may get entangled in relationships that neither enhance our spiritual path nor bring us closer to our twin flame.

INNER ONENESS *and* BLISS

Even if we are married to our twin flame and have known that one for many lifetimes, until we have contacted the heart fire and God-awareness of our twin flame, we have not been completely re-united. We may have had an outer union but not an inner union, and so we still don't have the fulfillment of oneness. This only comes when the fire leaps in our heart and we experience the deep eternal love of twin flames. Only then, through the spiritual union, will we have the oneness of the two joined as a whole.

The union of twin flames cannot be known until it is experienced. This doesn't necessarily mean that it is the most perfect relationship at the human level. But when twin flames are present with one another, there is a mutual reverence and a deep inner spiritual interchange.

"What therefore God hath joined together, let no man put asunder."[2] This statement can be understood in the light of twin flames. What God has joined together is twin flames. Conceived out of the same white-fire body, you and your twin flame are one. Nothing can separate this divine union at the spiritual level. No matter what the situation appears to be outwardly, twin flames are never separated at the level of the God Presence. Wherever the other half of the whole is, there is oneness.

The rejoicing in the heart of this oneness can be given by the mantra, "We are one!" When you give this mantra, you may realize that all separation, all that has kept you apart from your twin flame, comes to naught as you commune in the living flame of your love.

SOUL MEMORIES

Mark Prophet, my twin flame, began the lifelong quest that led to our meeting when he was very young. Many of us have had a memory of a divine counterpart and of this inner union. It may have been conscious, but more often it was not conscious, perhaps just a sense or an intuition. Mark's memory of higher realms remained with him always and he had conscious soul memories of our twin flames. He remembered that as a young child he had marvelous inner experiences with someone he would one day have a mission with.

Mark L. Prophet

Once I saw a scrapbook that Mark had made as a child. His mother was a student of the Unity Church, where she learned about treasure mapping, which is creating a visual representation of something you would like to bring into your life. She taught Mark about it, including the understanding that you should have pictures and write about whatever you want to bring forth. So Mark made his own scrapbook, and he cut out a picture he had found in a magazine of a boy who looked like himself and he put it on one page in the front of the scrapbook. Then he cut out a picture of a little girl about six years old and put it on the other page. This was his dream girl, and this little girl that he cut out looked exactly like I looked when I was six.

On some pages later in the scrapbook, I found a picture he had cut out when he was in the Air Force during the war, and it was a soldier with his bride looking over their home. This was the vision that he held for his future happiness, with his home and children. He had told me about these pictures that he had in this book and how I had fulfilled his dream of bringing him happiness, a home, and children, but I had never seen them before. I thought how interesting it was that he had magnetized me to him by maintaining this vision.

IDENTIFYING *the* ONE

There is something very precious about the moment when you first identify your twin flame, when you first see the image and the face in a vision or perhaps in the flesh, and suddenly you feel that contact. It is a contact with the part of life that you know to be one with your Real Self. This is a moment that no one can give you and that no one must take from you.

The first day I met Mark was at a meeting in Boston where he was speaking. I sat down in front of the small platform where he was seated, and I closed my eyes and began to meditate. As I did so, Mark opened his eyes and saw me sitting there. Later he told me that he recognized me at once as his twin flame.

But being young and not as advanced as he was on the spiritual path, nor realizing what twin flames were, nor having the search for the twin flame in the forefront of my mind, I did not experience the conscious impact of contacting my twin flame at that first meeting. I saw a teacher, one whom I could follow. And later, as I thought about the concept of a twin flame, I sought confirmation from God that I might truly know if this man was indeed mine.

So I asked God to show me, and he gave me two of the most astounding experiences of my life. One day, when I looked into a mirror that I was passing by, I saw not my face but the face of Mark. It was as though my whole face had taken on his features. I looked into that mirror and I beheld myself as my divine counterpart.

It's quite a shock to look in the mirror and not see your own face. Imagine the impact of this and then, beyond that, the realization that when you see the other half of the divine whole face-to-face, it's like seeing God face-to-face. For accompanying the vision was the spark and the God consciousness. I was breathless because I had experienced the action of my twin flame. And later on, perhaps some weeks or months later, I had a similar occurrence as I was passing a store window and saw myself as Mark reflected in that window.

THE INNER RECOGNITION

The inner recognition of our beloved may come in the most unexpected and tender ways. God loves to surprise us. In the following story, this woman stopped looking outwardly for her divine love, but she also followed her heart. And then she met her twin flame when she least expected.

I was a young college student when I first heard about the wonderful concept of twin flames. I thought that my twin flame was in heaven, so I decided that I would visualize being introduced to him in the heavenly realms. In my lively imagination, I fashioned a lovely meditation where my beloved and I waltzed away to beautiful music. This idea of meeting my twin flame in heaven was comforting, as was my meditation, and helped me surrender the idea of running around trying to find my twin flame on earth, which was a great relief, and also a great time-saver!

Later, after college, when I was at a social event that happened to have some waltz music, a handsome young man with velvet brown eyes, whom I did not remember ever seeing before, asked me to dance, and I said yes. I looked into his eyes and I felt like I was falling into a galaxy. I "recognized" him, not in the storybook love-at-first-sight kind of way, but with a much deeper soul connection. I knew he was The One. My mind was wondering how this was even possible since I was quite sure my twin flame was up in heaven. But my heart knew. He felt the same way, and later he told me that he knew I was the one for him because his heart burned when we danced.

We were married soon afterward, and I was grateful to have found him, for that instant recognition developed into a lasting love. We have been married for over twenty-

five years, and our connection is still as profound to me as
it was in the moment we met.

Over time and through a series of inner and outer
events, it became clear that we were indeed twin flames.
My waltz meditation had come true right here on earth!

The young teacher in the following story experienced a soul
recognition of his twin flame the very first time he heard her voice.
Not long afterwards, their deepening love was the unquestionable
confirmation.

In the early spring of 1965, I was in the United States
Army, stationed on a military base on the island of Hok-
kaido, in Japan, near its capital city of Sapporo. While I
was there I used much of my free time, as many G.I.s did,
teaching English conversation to Japanese young people
and adults. On the first day of a new semester, I always
liked to begin by asking each student to say his or her
name and one or two things about themselves that they
were comfortable sharing. When I heard one of the young
women say her name, her voice caught me by surprise. I
suddenly sat up, looked in her direction and asked, "What
did you say?" She became a little embarrassed but then
repeated her name. It wasn't my intention to embarrass
her and I was surprised at my reaction to the sound of her
voice because it didn't make sense. Now I know that what
happened was that my soul, recognizing her voice, knew
the specialness of the person who spoke as being my twin
flame. But at the time I had no real sense of what had
happened.

Over the next several weeks, I learned that this young
woman, whose name was Miki, came from a well-respected
family in Sapporo and had just graduated from a junior

college in Tokyo. As it was the custom in Japan, a number of us would go to a nearby coffee shop after class to talk and share experiences. As I got to know Miki, I found that I thoroughly enjoyed talking with her because she was very bright and she had a very good sense of humor. She was also beautiful.

On Memorial Day 1965 we had our first date, and that was the beginning of what became the most significant relationship in my life, that is until I began to understand my relationship to God and God's to me. I had met someone who was different from any other woman I had ever known, and I knew deeply that the friendship I had with Miki was profoundly special. I could not then have explained what was special about it; I just knew that it was. Talking with her, just being with her in a coffee shop, even with eight or nine other people, was a joyously remarkable and unique experience.

It was in November 1965 that we realized that in fact we had fallen in love with each other, and we got engaged before the end of the year. A few months later we discovered that she was fighting a chronic illness that prevented our pursuing a long-term future together. Nevertheless, we still had more than a year ahead to deepen our friendship and love before she passed away in March 1967.

I can still remember one afternoon after we had come to realize what we meant to each other. I looked at her and I thought, "I am really lucky to have been able to come to Japan and find this extraordinary and exquisite person. She makes me feel like I am one—like I am complete." I wasn't sure I could explain the feeling, but the feeling was clear and it was certain. Then I had a couple of odd thoughts: "Is Miki the most intelligent woman I have ever

known?" "No," I answered myself, "she isn't. And yet,
she is the most intelligent woman I have ever known."
I remember smiling and thinking, "Well, is she the most
beautiful woman I have ever seen?" I answered myself
silently, "No, I don't think she is; and yet, she is the most
beautiful woman I have ever seen."

THE ONGOING SEARCH

As long as I have been teaching, I have received hundreds of
letters from people who tell me that they have found their twin
flame. To identify their twin flame, at first they may look for certain
physical features and characteristics. This may come from the inner
knowledge of the true nature of the soul, in which there are no
karmic irregularities that manifest physically and the natural beauty
is outpictured. We tend to search for this archetype.

But frequently we also base our belief about who our twin
flame is on a human love experience, compatible personalities, or a
physical attraction. More often than not, these are external signs
that point to a soul-mate or karmic relationship rather than to twin
flames.

We tend to look for these outer signs. Therefore our concepts
may not be founded on an internal sense of the divine archetype, but
rather they may be based on a human ideal. For instance, in high
school a lot of boys may be enamored with the same one, two, or
three girls because they're very pretty and they seem to have the
attributes that everybody wants. And many of the girls may be
starry-eyed about just a few of the boys.

This emphasis on mere physical attractiveness can be a devastating experience because, like anyone, such people may be superficial and shallow. When we get involved with them, they may not
have the qualities, the character, the depth, or the ability to have a
loving relationship. Or they may simply not be anything like what

we imagined or wished for. It's easy to get entangled in such a relationship. It can be difficult or unfulfilling, and then it may end. Afterwards we may wonder what happened. Perhaps we feel that we have truly loved this person, but now we regret the relationship.

We can readily get confused by the perceptions of our outer mind. We may try to determine who our twin flame is by what we see as positive or negative qualities or other surface characteristics. Most people do have a collection of good and bad qualities, so these do not provide an accurate indication of whether or not someone is our twin flame.

Sometimes we may think that someone is our twin flame because that person is so much like us. Although this may seem logical, it is more likely that twin flames will be distinctly opposite because they have each realized the opposite side, one distinct half, of the divine whole. Having been separated for so long, they have developed different personalities. And they have engaged in misuses of energy and entanglements in the ways of the world, setting in motion their own karmic cycles. Therefore, they may not incarnate with the same habits and patterns that we have.

In the search for our twin flame, we may also assume that someone is our twin flame because we remember him* from a past life. The recollection of past lives with someone as a marriage partner or in other roles is not proof that that person is a soul mate or a twin flame. It's merely a recollection that we've known him before.

These ideas and expectations can trip us up in another way. Even when we meet our twin flame, we may have a fantasy about a love without imperfections. We may be so programmed, partially by the media and advertising, that we may feel that a meeting of our twin flame is a disappointment. For we have expectations from a superficial image of a physical flesh-and-blood prototype of who

---

*Because gender-neutral language can be cumbersome, we have often used *he* or *him* to refer to the individual. These terms are used for readability and are not intended to exclude women.

should be our counterpart and who we should marry. So sometimes we ignore the most beautiful part of another because we are looking at something else.

A PRACTICAL APPROACH *to* FINDING YOUR TWIN FLAME

We can develop an attraction to our twin flame, to a soul mate, or to anyone else. We have had experiences in many lifetimes that influence us to feel attracted to people we meet throughout our life, including experiences involving karma. Therefore before we find our twin flame, we are likely to have other attractions and feel inclined to engage in a number of relationships.

However, we only have so much time and energy in a given life, so we have to decide what relationships to pursue. If we're in a relationship that is not productive, harmonious, or contributing to the spiritual path of each one, we could miss our twin flame. Also, if we harbor within ourselves records of grief, fear, or nonforgiveness of our twin flame from past lives, these may be blocks to uniting with him, and they may influence us to seek other relationships.

If we want to find our twin flame, we can consciously and specifically direct our attention to that goal. We can write down the best qualities that we sense would be embodied by our other half. In addition, we can write down the goal of the relationship once we find our twin flame and what we want to accomplish in this lifetime. For within twenty, fifty, seventy-five, or a hundred years, all of us will have lived this life and we will be looking back at what we have done to serve others. The accomplishment is not finding your twin flame. The accomplishment is what you do the day after.

You can create a physical illustration, or treasure map, of your twin flame, just like Mark did. First, collect pictures that represent your twin flame. Then paste them onto green paper or poster board. Green represents abundance, the abundance of God's gifts in whatever form they may take. You can also add statements of affirmations or qualities. Be as specific as possible in your details, such as how the person looks, their personality, and so forth. You can even add the date that you would like to see your vision manifest. All of this is goal fitting.

Define the reason for the relationship. Tell God why you want the perfect mate in your life. Tell him that no matter what kind of relationship it is, above and beyond all, you want to do his will.

Then look at this treasure map a few times every day, including, perhaps, the first thing in the morning and at the end of the day. As you do, give this vision to your Higher Self and ask for God's will, trusting that all will be fulfilled in divine order. Finally, imagine that the relationship is happening right now and that this person is in your life bringing you joy and a higher love that satisfies the longing of your soul.

Meanwhile, be open to the gifts that may come to you in response to your heartfelt attention. It may be that what your soul needs is something different than what you envision. Your focus and your faith will bring you exactly what you need for your understanding and growth.

THE INNER MAGNET
THAT DRAWS YOU TOGETHER

One of the reasons we are separated from our beloved is because we lack internal wholeness, and cosmic law compels us to manifest some portion of this wholeness before we encounter our twin flame. As we seek this wholeness in God, we will magnetize more wholeness in ourself.

As a young woman in college and seeking God intensely, I was certain that no man would have me because of my desire for God. While I wanted to consider marriage, I had put aside the idea of finding the perfect relationship. I was healed of the need for it when

I sought the answer in God and in sacred scripture. With a sense of receptivity to whatever God would show me, I let the Bible fall open where it would. When it did, my eyes landed upon these uplifting words, "For, lo, thy Maker is thine husband."[3] And it was as though I experienced a burst of conscious awareness. I said, "Yes, I am wed to God. God is my husband. God fulfills all my needs."

It was the spiraling of energy from my soul to my God Presence, and I felt whole. I felt the bliss of union with God. That understanding carried me through many years of service as my consciousness increased in its awareness of the whole. At the time that I reached a certain intensity of this awareness, Mark appeared in my life. From among the millions of people in the millions of places across the planet, we found ourselves at the same time in one place, meeting for the first time in this life. Because I was aware of my inner wholeness, I had attracted the counterpart of my identity.

Following is a story of two people who also decided to stop looking for their other half and to pursue the spiritual path instead, with a surprising outcome.

The dream was almost always the same. I was at a dance and I saw a girl sitting by herself against a wall as if she was waiting for someone. I recognized her but I didn't know who she was. I was filled with a great love and happiness that was hard to describe and then, invariably, I would awaken and realize it was only a dream. Or was it?

Throughout college and in my twenties, I was searching spiritually for the elusive love that I yearned for. My search seemed successful when, after college, I went to East Africa and met a girl who shared my spiritual goals and interests. Yet even though I hoped she was the one, an inner sense told me that she was not. I pursued a number of relationships, but I never felt the quickening or confirmation in my heart. So I was beginning to doubt that I would ever find her.

Then I decided to stop looking and to focus on my spiritual path. Unknown to me, halfway around the world in Latin America, a young woman in her early twenties was traveling, working, and searching spiritually for many answers. Even though we were physically as far apart as two people could be, we were linked by our search for God.

By and by, about three years later, we met in a most unexpected time and place—in a very large city that was foreign to both of us. God had to give me a little prompting and if I hadn't obeyed I would likely have missed her. On the surface we were opposites in many ways, yet during the days and weeks of talking and sharing, the deeper inner connection became stronger.

I have no need to dream of her anymore since we have been married for many years. Putting God first has always been our priority. Our spiritual journey brought us together, filled our lives with love, a joyful family, fruitful work, and helped us navigate every challenge. Because our journey seems to get better and better, we often say to one another, "The best is yet to come!"

TWIN FLAMES APART

Sometimes two people are twin flames and they know this at a soul level. However, it's possible that they are not meant to be together in this life. In such instances, often the outer mind is not consciously aware of what the soul knows at the subconscious level, and this could be a protection for all involved.

When twin flames are not meant to be together in their current life, it could be for a number of reasons. Perhaps the reestablishment of the twin-flame relationship would mean breaking up families and homes. Or it would cause cataclysm in people's lives because they are in situations that are binding, for instance they are working on past karma that needs to be resolved before they move on in life.

It can happen that two individuals who are twin flames are each married to someone else. These twin flames may know one another and even see each other in their normal day-to-day activities, perhaps in their jobs. But they happily maintain their marriages even as they have a healthy working relationship or friendship with the person who is their twin flame (though they do not recognize the twin flame in their outer awareness).

I have seen twin flames where the man was twenty and the woman was seventy. Not surprisingly, their meeting did not produce instant love and marriage. Nor did the relationship become anything more than a loyal friendship and a mutual fondness. In fact, though inseparable, they never even realized they were twin flames. It wasn't necessary for them to know. Their souls knew, and they accomplished what they were supposed to do without having to deal with any more than they were ready for.

When it's obvious that the divine plan is not to meet your twin flame, that doesn't mean that God won't provide a partner, a companion, a husband or a wife. This person may be a soul mate, someone whom you have been good friends with for a long time, whom you care for deeply, with whom you can get a job done—a relationship that is soul-satisfying because it's project oriented. Or you may have karma that cannot be balanced any other way than in a marriage, and that too may be fulfilling for the lessons that you learn and for the love you give to one another and your children, which is all-important.

TOGETHER *at* LAST—WHAT'S NEXT?

Sharing a relationship with one's twin flame is a most blessed and sacred opportunity. It's a time of rejoicing after many lifetimes of being apart, and yet there can be challenges, as in any other relationship. So just meeting our twin flame doesn't necessarily mean that everything is going to be wonderful. Having embodied all over the earth in various lifetimes and circumstances and having created many karmic conditions, twin flames may easily have superficial personality clashes or other difficulties. When we understand that these things are not the true essence of our relationship, we can work through them. In fact, there are no twin flames on the planet who are karma-free with one another, and therefore part of the task of twin flames is to balance their karma.

In the case of Mark and me, I realized clearly that the intensity of our relationship was great, and therefore it was also delicate. Due to the inner pain and sorrow of having been separated for so long as well as having made karma, twin flames often do experience a great intensity in their relationship. This calls for thoughtful care, for without it significant discord can arise. Therefore it can be helpful for twin flames to recognize that their love can be much greater than any of the things that come between them.

Throughout the years I have had the privilege of talking with couples whom I know, from inner levels, to be twin flames. It's interesting to hear their common themes, which I can relate to through my own experience in being married to my twin flame. No other relationship on this earth even comes close to comparing. It is the feeling of inner oneness that sets these relationships apart. This woman described such an experience when she told me about her marriage to her twin flame.

> *Our marriage is happy, but we have our differences, just like any other couple. We are very different people. We have different interests and we're opposite in many ways. But there is always a feeling of deep inner connectedness. My husband is so much a part of myself at inner levels that it's just a fact. This feeling of inner connectedness has never changed since our first moment of recognition, and we have been married for almost thirty*

*years. This is what carries us through all of the differences
and difficulties that come up.*

*Sometimes situations and feelings arise that can be
really deep, but we know that we can't just walk away
from them. They must be resolved, and the only way out
is to go forward. Sometimes this is as simple as talking the
issue through, and sometimes it requires being on our
knees in deep prayer.*

*It feels like these deep issues have to do with the point
of original departure from one another. It is much deeper
than the surface drama that is going on. Sometimes I'm
afraid I will lose him again, but at the same time I know
that this is an irrational fear. Yet it is intense. But no matter
what the problem is, there is a feeling of inner oneness
between us that makes it our greatest desire to resolve
these intense issues.*

I often find that twin flames are so different that they provide
a good balance for one another. One may be calm and centered
while the other is more passionate and emotional. When one is
upset, the other brings a sense of peace. They learn from each other.
One may enjoy physical work, while the other is more intellectually
driven. Regardless of the differences, twin flames share a tremendous love that is the creative energy of God.

Since you are one with your twin flame, you can ask: What will
we do with this tremendous love? What are we going to achieve?
How can we balance our karma and share our love with the world?

You can share this deep love if you are with your soul mate,
your twin flame or in a karmic marriage. What matters is that you
and your partner share a real giving of self, a pure loving, and an
accomplishment of some lasting good.

A PRAYER *to* SERVE *with* YOUR TWIN FLAME

Whether you are with your twin flame or not, you can give the following pledge of twin flames to balance karma and serve in harmony. You can handwrite the prayer, then sign and date it, and place it in your Bible or in another holy book:

> O God, I desire to perform the best service and to fulfill my inner vow with my twin flame. If it be that karma does separate us and therefore our service, I pray to you to set it aside for an hour and a year that we might show ourselves worthy, plow the straight furrow, and enter into the service of God and our fellow man. Thus, we pray that together we may choose to balance that karma. And we do choose to do so, O God.

THE EXPANSIVE LOVE *of* TWIN FLAMES

The fire of your heart can fuse with the fire of the heart of your twin flame, and this is eternal love. You sense the oneness; you are not alone. (See Plate 3.) You walk around feeling joyous, all-one, by God's all-consuming joy flame, in the giving of yourself to God in his own. This love, which is born out of your wholeness, is so wonderful, so full of wonder, that you can never stop giving it and never stop being refilled. It cheats no one else, neither your present spouse nor your children nor your friends, but it is a love that can embrace all. This love of twin flames, which gives profound and everlasting meaning to life, can only multiply your love for everyone else.

Right now, your love for your twin flame can bring joy and fullness, purpose in living, whether you are together or apart. It can be a love like the love of newlyweds, where the whole world is full of your love and everyone you meet receives the love of two hearts that beat as one as you forge this union more beautifully day by day.

This twin-flame love carries an intensity that can be translated into the productive work of the hour and service to others. If you are with your twin flame in this life, you have the opportunity to expand this blessing of your union. You have a great love to share as well as the power and creative energy of the universe. You can ponder what magnificent creation you are going to bring forth and lay upon the altar of humanity so that, by your love, the whole human race is elevated. For ultimately that is the reason God made you twin flames.

And everything positive that you do right now is also helping you and your twin flame to balance your joint karma so that you can come to the point of the grand reunion, which, in a sense, is only the beginning. You and your twin flame are destined to move on through the ages, through the light of cosmos, to expand the consciousness of the Father-Mother God. For God is continually transcending. God continually becomes more of God. There is no end to the possibilities. And once you are free of the chains of karma and the rounds of rebirth, you will be free to fulfill your destiny— together, worlds without end.

The story of Winston Churchill and his twin flame, Clementine, reveals the depth of their twin-flame love, which was the fount from which they drew to provide a great service to their country.

> *Nothing could separate Winston Churchill and his beloved, Clementine, or diminish their love. Without consciously knowing they were twin flames, they shared an intense loyalty and commitment. While their outer relationship had challenges and was not perfect, the divine interchange between them was profound. Uniquely different, they provided the perfect complement for one another. Clementine held a calm and intense love and support that enabled Churchill to valiantly lead at a time of grave world crisis and war.*

*By the time he met Clem-
entine, Winston Churchill had
written numerous books, served
in Parliament, and was famous
for his war-time exploits on
three continents. He had some
romantic interests but none that
lasted. Clementine was different
and he knew it. Yes, she was
beautiful, sensitive, and intelligent, but there was something
else about her. Probably not
consciously aware of what it
was, he had found his twin
flame. After a brief courtship,
they were married in 1908 and
only grew in love during their fifty-six years together.*

Winston and Clementine Churchill

*It was not an easy marriage. They were apart for
extended periods of time, through two world wars and
some of the greatest crises of the twentieth century. They
lost a young child, and an adult daughter committed sui-
cide. Yet their love endured. They left over seventeen hundred letters and other correspondence between them, and
the sweetness and purity of their love shines forth in language we would think quaint today.*

*When we think of Churchill, the image is often of an
embattled war leader inspiring a nation and a world to rise
up and defeat an evil that threatened us all. He was that
and more, but he was also a devoted husband who could
write to his Clementine words such as this:*

*"I do not love and will never love any woman in the
world but you.... Beloved, I kiss your memory—Your sweetness and beauty have cast a glory upon my life. You will*

find me always your loving and devoted husband."[4]

Could Winston have accomplished so much without the love and support of his dear Clementine that sustained him through some of the most perilous and darkest days of history? His accomplishments were not entirely his own, but they were also the fruit of the powerful love of twin flames.

ALL LOVE RETURNS *to* YOUR TWIN FLAME

Through the ups and downs of relationships, we all have experienced times when love was not returned to us in the way we hoped. Nevertheless, we need not feel that we have failed because we have loved without response.

For the love that is a fountain in your heart, the love that swells up as it flows, can never be stopped, because it comes from God. It returns to God. It originates in the source of your being and it returns to that source. And in the process of going forth and returning to the source, it must merge with and cycle through the consciousness of your twin flame. Therefore all the love that you have ever given to anyone, anywhere, always returns to the heart of your twin flame.

In a sense, it doesn't matter to whom you are married. It matters in that you will be married to the one with whom you are required to serve by your karma, and that marriage always commemorates the union of twin flames. Whether or not you are married to your twin flame, you are married in the service of your twin flame. You are married to give love, while preparing yourself to meet your twin flame.

To love and to continue to love and to love more, whether or not the object of that love is your twin flame, whether that one is deserving in your sight, is the way of the spiritual path. For God is always worthy of your love and God lives in the hearts of all people.

So you can truthfully say when you look upon your child, upon your beloved, upon your father or mother or friend, "O God, you are so magnificent! I love you, I love you, I love you." And by speaking to God in man, in woman, and in child, you invoke God, and that one will be God receiving your love. This is the homeward path. For true love is not self-seeking. It is loving for the sake of loving.

CHAPTER 3

SOUL MATES

*N*ot all of the beautiful and soul-fulfilling love relationships are those of twin flames. Many are the loves of close, kindred souls called soul mates.

Soul mates have a similar soul development and path of self-mastery. They come together because they're working on balancing the same type of karma and developing similar qualities, and they tend to be complimentary. They are mates in the sense of being partners for the journey, very much alike and compatible because their soul development is at the same level. In a soul-mate marriage the couple often works together to provide a mutual service, balance karma, and fulfill their purpose in life.

You will have a number of such associations throughout your lifetimes. And even if you are with your twin flame in your current lifetime, you are likely to have others in your life who are your soul mates. A boyfriend or girlfriend, a husband or wife could be a soul mate. But many others, possibly coworkers or friends, could also be soul mates.

Soul mates may be the same or different ages. Frequently they have similar facial features and a similar type of physique. The various kinds of soul-mate relationships often have a great harmony and a certain element of completeness. Therefore soul mates can have strong, healthy marriages, friendships, and brother-sister or other family relationships.

Soul-mate relationships can be less intense than twin-flame relationships because soul mates don't have the same pain of the original separation from their divine partner and the subsequent lifetimes of being apart. While they're separated, twin flames may create a lot of negative karma, which could make their relationship more difficult and cause friction between them. So sometimes soul mates feel closer to one another than twin flames do.

SHARING *a* DUAL SERVICE

A soul mate may be a person you have worked with on the same mission for many lifetimes. Oftentimes the two of you work well together and are project oriented. Because of your similarities, you may have parallel interests and aptitudes.

For instance, in this lifetime your choice as well as your assignment could be to master music. If so, you may be assembled with many musicians, and you may find someone who is very much a coworker and a companion with whom you can share not only your love of harmony but also a real soul communion. You can also share an extra blessing, the blessing that comes to you and your endeavors from the God Presence of both of your twin flames—your twin flame and your soul mate's twin flame. This extra blessing amplifies the constructive potential of soul mates united in work or service.

A partnership that reflected the relationship of soul mates sharing a dual service was the marriage of John Adams, the second president of the United States, and his wife Abigail.

*The more than eleven hundred letters between John
and Abigail Adams often began with the words "My Dearest Friend."[1] From their correspondence, it is clear that
these soul mates could never have accomplished alone
what they did together. It was a marriage of equals with a
common goal. They had many long separations, and in
their frequent letters Abigail added encouragement, insight, and perspective to the multitude of issues John was
facing in his political life.*

*Abigail's astute observations and her native intelli-
gence were the perfect sounding board for John. For example, in March 1776, when he was writing laws, she
challenged him to "remember the ladies and be more gen-
erous and favorable to them than your ancestors." She
continued: "[We] will not hold ourselves bound by any
laws in which we have no voice or representation."[2]
Through their joint efforts, they were united in their devotion to God and to freedom in revolutionary America.*

*John and Abigail believed that "the purpose of life
was to serve, to perform acts of virtue and generosity, to
sacrifice for the community and for the improvement of
the world."[3] And sacrifice they did. They put their personal lives second to their higher calling together. John
wrote, "She never by work or look discouraged me from
running all hazards for the salvation of my country's lib-
erties; she was willing to share with me...in all the dan-
gerous consequences we had to hazard."[4]*

The cause of freedom owes a great deal to these souls, who
accomplished so much because of the mutual recognition of their
calling. It was, undoubtedly, one of the greatest partnerships in
American history.

The mission of John and Abigail Adams made enough of an
imprint upon history that they became known far beyond the borders

of their immediate world. However, other soul mates who are less prominent in the world often work side by side in their quiet but significant service to life, like the young man and woman in the following story.

I was working in a Hebrew school on the East Coast. In addition to teaching, I also wrote children's stories about the prophets and leaders of the Old Testament. I loved my job and was totally immersed in it, so I wasn't even thinking much about men or marriage.

Then a new teacher came to work there, but I didn't think much about it. He, too, was fascinated by the figures in the Bible and he created beautiful, colorful slide shows about their lives to inspire the children. Soon after he began teaching at the school, somehow I often found myself around him, though I didn't plan it that way. I had had some bad experiences with men, so frankly I was a little bit afraid of them. Therefore I tried to avoid this man, but he quietly entered my life. I began to notice how tender and sweet he was. Meanwhile, I found out later, he was in a quandary. He was beginning to have feelings of love for me, but I seemed so standoffish and disinterested that he didn't know what to do because he didn't want to force himself on me.

Finally he decided to just ask me out to see what would happen. One Sunday morning we went on our first outing together. We had a picnic in a little grove of trees not far from the school. It was a quiet meeting; we were both a little shy. But as I was sitting in his presence, I had a sense of joy, peace, and even just the tiniest bud of love.

In due time we married. The little bud of love blossomed into a perpetual bouquet. We both continued teaching at the Hebrew school and creating stories in written and visual form about the notable men and women in the

Old Testament. We never had any children, but we consider our work and service as our children. Our marriage has been happy, harmonious, and extremely blessed. And even to this day, I still feel the same joy, peace, and love that I felt on that very first day when we had our picnic together in the little grove of trees.

The mutual and complementary service of these teachers as well as their natural reciprocal relationship exemplifies the nature of a soul-mate relationship. The harmony and easiness in being together is also a sign of a relationship with two people who probably have much positive karma and a minimum of negative karma. It shows how soul mates can have a supportive and productive relationship, and this can occur with marriage partners, various family relationships, coworkers, or friends.

BROTHER *and* SISTER *at* HEART

Soul mates can be partners who truly love and respect one another. Though they may share a strong attraction and bond and have fulfilling marriages and a deep union of hearts, ultimately their relationship is more like a brother and sister, with that element of congruity and companionship.

While you and your soul mate may love each other deeply, you may sense that such a relationship does not go as high and is not as profound as the relationship with your divine counterpart—the twin flame who has been your other half from the first moment of your creation. Therefore although the soul-mate relationship may have many elements of romance, it is not the ultimate divine romance of the soul with her twin flame.

However, sometimes people assume that just because they have found a soul mate, they are meant to have a romantic involvement with that person. When you find one person or more with whom you connect for the accomplishment of a worthwhile endeavor, you may indeed be soul mates, but that does not mean that it is automatically intended to be a romantic relationship. In fact, one may complete the project and be ready for the next step in life, which can involve an entirely new circle of people and perhaps another soul mate.

PRAYERS *to* STRENGTHEN *and* PROTECT RELATIONSHIPS

As we now know, our soul has lived through a long history of encounters, entanglements, and separations involving our twin flame, soul mates, and others. Throughout these times and in these relationships, we have experienced setbacks and problems as well as obstacles to finding our highest love.

Therefore you may find that you want to strengthen and protect your relationships, and you can give your heartfelt prayers to God for this purpose. For an effective reinforcement of your devotions, you can use what I call the science of the spoken Word, which is a form of spoken prayer.

Spoken prayer is at the heart of the world's religions, as many of us have experienced in our own lives. The science of the spoken Word is a step-up of the prayer forms of both East and West. It involves using prayers, mantras, affirmations, and meditations along with dynamic decrees—powerful spoken petitions to God.

When we meditate, we commune with God. When we pray, we communicate with God and request his help. When we decree, we are communing, communicating, and directing God's light into our world to change the circumstances we see around us. We are, in effect, commanding the flow of energy from Spirit to matter.

USING *the* SCIENCE *of the* SPOKEN WORD

Many decrees and affirmations use the name of God "I AM" to access spiritual power. "I AM" is the name of God revealed to

Moses when he saw the burning bush. "I AM THAT I AM" means "as above, so below"—"as God is in heaven, so God is on earth within me. The power of God is right where I stand." Every time you say, "I AM...," you are affirming, "God in me is...."

As you may know, ancient spiritual traditions as well as modern scientific studies have shown that sound is effective in creating change. So when we want to draw down the light and energy of God for transformation and for positive change in the world at large, giving decrees aloud is indispensable.

In addition, we can enhance the power of our prayers when we specifically name and visualize what we want to take place. Whatever we put our attention on we are charging with energy. The image we hold in our mind's eye is like a blueprint, and our attention is the magnet that attracts the creative energies of Spirit to fill in that blueprint with what we want to manifest.

Repetition also increases the benefits of spoken prayer. Decrees, fiats, and mantras are all meant to be repeated. In the East people give their mantras over and over, even thousands of times a day. But in the West we are usually not accustomed to doing this. Sometimes people say, "Why should I have to ask God for something more than once?" The answer is that repeating a prayer is not simply making a request again and again. In truth, it is strengthening the power of the request by qualifying it with more of God's light-energy.

You can also ask God to send his angels to protect you. Thousands of people have experienced miracles that they believe were made possible by their prayers to the angels. The greatest and most revered angel in Jewish, Christian, and Islamic traditions is Archangel Michael. (See Plate 4.) He and the legions of angels he commands protect us from physical and spiritual dangers. Archangel Michael has personally saved my life a dozen times that I know of and probably thousands of times that I am not aware of. I am sure that the same is true for you.

A decree can be used for anything positive that you would like to bring about for yourself and your relationships and for you and your twin flame. You can give a prayer to God to protect your twin flame and your finding each other if it is your divine plan in this life. In any prayer or decree you give, you can also include the address "Beloved God Presence and Higher Self of myself and my beloved twin flame...."

When you want to call to Archangel Michael to assist you, visualize him as a beautiful, powerful, and majestic angel arrayed in shining armor, with a brilliant sapphire blue cape and aura. See him standing before you, behind you, to your right, to your left, above, beneath, and all around you. He is always accompanied by limitless numbers of angels who will protect and escort you wherever you go.

> Lord* Michael before,
> Lord Michael behind,
> Lord Michael to the right,
> Lord Michael to the left,
> Lord Michael above,
> Lord Michael below,
> Lord Michael, Lord Michael wherever I go!
>
> I AM his love protecting here!
> I AM his love protecting here!
> I AM his love protecting here!

QUESTIONS & ANSWERS
with Elizabeth Clare Prophet on

Twin Flames and Soul Mates

MEETING *and* RECOGNIZING YOUR TWIN FLAME

Q: What's the feeling in my heart that will tell me if someone is my twin flame?

A: Most of us want to know the truth and to operate at the highest level of our own ability to perceive, and the most we can do is to enhance what I call *perceptors*. The greatest perceptor is the heart. If you want to experience the refined perception of your heart, you may need to purify and clear your heart of illusions, fantasies, and other unrealities. Purity of heart helps us to get through the challenges of life. Are your reasons pure? Is your motive pure? Is your desire pure? If you have that purity of heart, then your heart is a good receptor and you will receive the pure message.

But if you don't perceive right away or you're not certain about your perception, it's best to wait to make a decision or take any action. You can also ask God for confirmation and be open to the response.

Q: Does it matter if I don't meet my twin flame?

A: You know, our life plans are very complex. We descend into life with a certain job to do. We have many accounts to settle and responsibilities we haven't fulfilled from other lifetimes. And sometimes we have to get through a lot of those things before the cycle comes for us to meet our twin flame.

Sometimes it's the boy next door. You may have known him all your life, but you had to get everything else out of the way first, a certain amount of karma, before you could recognize him. It's so different for everyone. Sometimes it's imperative that you find your twin flame and sometimes it's not the plan for this life.

In any case, remember that, in a sense, whoever you are with is your twin flame because anyone can be the vessel of God. Anybody you meet can be the friend, the teacher, or the instrument of the Higher Self.

So we love one another as we love our twin flame in the spiritual sense, and by exercising that givingness to all kinds of people—not just in male-female relationships but with children and everyone else we meet—we're practicing the presence of love. And beyond the person we know, we're sending love to our twin flame. And that's what is important, that we exercise love in life.

Q: **How can I speed up meeting my twin flame?**

A: The more you can get through cycles of past causes you've set in motion, the more you can speed up your life. And when I say "get through," I mean to transmute, or transform, and resolve. By using specific spiritual prayers and affirmations for this purpose, you can do more in this lifetime than you could in previous lives under ordinary circumstances. (See Chapter 5 on the violet flame.)

You can also write letters to God; they work. Just write a letter and place it in your Bible or in another holy book and put it where you pray or meditate. Then ask God, if it is his will and in accordance with your divine plan, to please reveal your twin flame, and ask him how you can work together at inner or outer levels with that person.

You know, God loves to do things for us. He loves to make

us happy. And it's nice to be able to wait for the reward, to give God the opportunity to do something for us. We can do this by being diligent in what we're supposed to be doing in developing ourselves, growing in love, and serving others. If we try to get things for ourselves that we should be waiting to receive through God's grace, it takes the joy out of God spontaneously giving us surprises in life.

THE UPS *and* DOWNS *of* TWIN-FLAME RELATIONSHIPS

Q: **Will twin flames share a more-than-ordinary romantic relationship?**

A: Not necessarily. While twin flames share a profound inner union, sometimes the relationship of twin flames is as difficult as any marriage or partnership in life. And unless each person is willing to surrender and put aside the challenging things for the greater love, twin flames can divorce as easily as other people.

Twin-flame relationships, like others, can be influenced and complicated by unreasonable expectations. Many of us have unrealistic notions of romantic love because of what we've seen in the media for decades. These ideas lead us to expect perfection and to expect that our mate will fulfill all of our needs and desires, to expect that marriage will be simply beyond this world in bliss. This is partly why we can experience extreme disappointments and frustrations in all kinds of relationships.

We expect our partner to be father and mother and all things to us instead of entering the relationship with an expectancy of giving again and again and seeing it as a path of challenges and learning—a path whereby the rough spots in each one become evident and we have the opportunity to work through them. In reality, we need to be willing to work on ourselves and to also hold the vision for our mate and help that one to overcome.

Twin flames especially need compassion for each other. For the depth of soul pain from being separated from one another for so long can surface extreme passions and emotions. The point of the relationship is resolution and the sharing of love, the ennobling of life, the uplifting of God's kingdom, and ultimately the highest union of your love.

Q: **What if twin flames are on different levels on the spiritual path?**

A: If the other person is more advanced than you are, perhaps having a deeper spiritual understanding, you have a great opportunity. You can draw forth more light and it can be exalting.

If you are the one who is more advanced, you may be carrying a heavier burden than you realize. Although you may not know your twin flame, you may be carrying the burden of someone who is bowed down, for instance if your twin flame is immersed in the drug culture, living in poverty, or very sick.

In other words, your twin flame may be in a difficult situation, and therefore what he is going through can be pulling you down. You may not know why your life is a struggle, but it could be that somewhere on the planet your twin flame is having a hard time and you are holding a love for that person and helping to carry the weight of what he is going through.

Part of the journey back to God includes these concerns for those we care about, whether it is a twin flame or someone else. And this brings out the tremendous love that we can share. So you bless life and care for the life of those you know, whether it is your partner, the little children, or the aged. And you never know when you are reaching the point of loving the God in your other half, your twin flame.

Q: **Why do I feel resentment towards my twin flame and what should I do about it? After recently learning about twin flames, I started sending love to my twin flame and I noticed I had feelings of cynicism and resentment.**

A: Well, since you were in the mode of directing love to your twin flame and you felt resentment, it illustrates the fact that we have karma with our twin flame. We can have terrific resentment in our being toward something our twin flame did to us ten embodiments ago, and we could have been compensating for that experience for a number of lifetimes.

You can see that what you have been through may be the kind of resentment that says, "I'll show you. I'll show you that I can live without you. I can do what I want to do and I can have fun without you." It's where we're letting our resentment of one particular human experience prevent us from the divine union, while if we could accept it, we would be able to heal all the other things that may have occurred.

Now, put aside the twin-flame relationship and think about your life and loving someone—a parent, a child, a friend. You might know that the love is there, but you might have a problem, a resentment or something that is bothering you. And you can watch a love be destroyed because there was not the will to put down that sense of nonforgiveness, that sense of holding on to the resentment: "You did this to me; therefore, I will not allow this love to grow and bloom."

I would suggest that you just accept that perhaps something happened for which you feel resentment. You start with the melting of the heart with forgiveness. Forgive yourself first. Then send forgiveness to your twin flame. You have wronged; your twin flame has wronged. It works both ways. I think you've come upon a very fundamental block on the spiritual path in this life, and if you pursue that forgiveness, you'll be free from a great burden.

PREPARATION and PROTECTION for the
TWIN-FLAME RELATIONSHIP

Q: **How can I avoid karma-making relationships as I strive for reunion with my twin flame?**

A: Well, if you're looking for your twin flame, you might decide to be one-pointed. Sometimes when someone else is occupying the space, the person you're meant to be with doesn't have room to come into your life. Sometimes you have to create a vacuum if you want the vacuum to be filled. Relationships can create a closed circuit.

If you're carrying on another relationship while you're looking for your twin flame, you're not really being honest in that relationship. You're not really giving pure love to that person. And the purpose of relationships is to give love to the person and to God. So you should either settle down with a person who is complementary to you and make a go of your life, or if this twin flame idea is important to you, then you may decide to wait. Everyone is different.

On the other hand, focusing on the idea of the twin flame can interfere with what's happening here and now in your life. The twin flame is at the highest level of the white-fire body of your God Presence, and this is the other half of the spiritual being that you were in the beginning. That person is already a part of you. Spiritually you are already one. But you may never meet in this life, or you might meet tomorrow. So you have to decide to be practical about your life in the meantime.

THIRD PARTIES

Q: **What should I do if my twin flame is already married to some-one else?**

A: You walk in the other direction. If you're thinking about a particular instance, you do have to realize that attractions are a dime a dozen in life. This person may not be your twin flame. Attractions are always with us, given the many types of circumstances we experience. But one doesn't base relationships on mere attractions. One bases them on the more profound things in life.

You may be experiencing something with this man, even at an emotional level, that is not rightfully yours to experience because it belongs exclusively to the one who holds the office of wife. If this is the case, then obviously you are the one who doesn't belong in the picture.

Therefore, you remove yourself from the scene. And if, independent of and apart from you, at some point the husband in this situation is no longer with that person, it becomes a different matter. But you should never be the reason that a marriage is brought to an end.

If you can't maintain a lawful contact with this man, then cutting off the contact gives the opportunity for his marriage to succeed. And you can move on and form other relationships. As long as the unlawful tie exists, it's displacing the fruitfulness and honor of their married relationship. Those who have taken the marriage vow have a commitment and a responsibility to their spouse and to maintaining the integrity of their marriage.

Q: Can somebody who has a strong magnetic pull tear twin flames apart?

A: There are many factors that can draw you away from your twin flame. The story in Homer's *Odyssey* of the siren on the rock and the mariners being irresistibly drawn to the siren relates to the fact that by the use of the sexual force as a magnet and by the process of physical allurement, twin flames have been enticed away from each other and their mission or divine plan.

This is one of the all-time great karmas of twin flames, that by the inordinate desire for more in the sexual experience than is lawful in God, one may cast aside the lawful relationship and the divine relationship. (See Chapter 7.)

The protection of twin flames from sexual attractions and temptations as they are portrayed on television, in movies, in advertising, and on the Internet is important. There's something very unreal about the portrayal of men and woman in the media, which has led people to have a super expectancy of the sexual encounter. Therefore normal sex isn't even in style in many places on the planet today, and that is a trap. It's a very unfortunate trap.

WHO COULD IT BE?

Q: Could my identical twin be my twin flame? Also, are twins often twin flames or soul mates?

A: Not necessarily. Twins have a very close karma to work out. Being in the womb at the same time is an amazing experience, but many times it's a love tie of brothers or sisters or just souls who have such a deep personal commitment to each other that they don't want to be separated. They could be soul mates in the sense that we've defined it, such as having a project to do together, or they could be twin flames.

I had an interesting experience in Washington of meeting an elderly man and woman who were twins by birth. They were also twin flames, but the woman was married. She had the most wonderful, happy brother-sister relationship with her twin, and she also had a wonderful relationship with her husband. In this life these twin flames played the roles of brother and sister, and they were not conscious of being twin flames. It was just very clear in their auras that they were twin flames.

Many twins have the sense of being very close, but they're not all twin flames. Because of some past karmic destiny, they may need to be twins, to share the womb, and to have many similar traits, according to their heredity. Obviously they are not destined to marry one another.

Q: Could my mother be my twin flame?

A: It has happened in history that twin flames have been mother and son or other kinds of relationships. However, it is important to be careful not to dwell on this, whether it is true or not.

It doesn't matter whether or not your mother is your twin flame. It's important that you mature to the point of being able to provide a strong identity and a wholeness to bring to the person that God has ordained for you in marriage if marriage is meant for you in this life. Entertaining that fantasy could be an avoidance of your responsibilities to go out and face the sometimes fearful situation of rejection or even acceptance from a member of the opposite sex.

Sometimes by fantasy itself we are in a position of a spiritual compromise. Although it is not a physical situation, it may become a spiritual crossing of the barrier.

For instance, it would not be lawful for me to entertain the concept that my father or my son were my twin flame. And if they were, the matter should be sealed because there are boundaries as to the types of relationships that we are allowed to have. Although someone may be our twin flame, it may not be lawful for us to have a twin-flame relationship with that person in the physical plane.

The family is a divine matrix in which each person plays a unique role in relation to others in that family unit. Through these roles there is a natural flow of love, a security, a strength, and a protection. These roles would override a twin-flame relationship between members of the family, except of course the parents.

Role playing can become more important than the issue of twin flames. And if it's the role for you to be the son and for your mother to be the mother, then you both play those roles. That is the role you play and you don't put any other connotations on it, even mentally. The son is the son. Father is father. Daughter is daughter. And there's a sanctity to these relationships and offices. So one must mature to the place of being capable of delivering love and receiving love in the appropriate manner.

THE DIVINE POLARITY

Q: **What determines which sex, or gender, you are born with?**

A: Your karma determines what sex your body is. Your soul never changes. Your soul is your soul and your Higher Self is your Higher Self.

So you are far more than your physical gender. Yet your karma, the lessons you need to learn and the relationships you need to have, determine which body you wear. So we do have masculine and feminine lifetimes because one of our tests is to develop both male and female qualities. The ultimate goal of your soul's wholeness and reunion with the twin flame requires the balancing and mastering of both facets of your energy. And so your sex is not an accident of biology.

Therefore you are born with the sex that will provide the opportunities for the lessons you need to learn. If you are a female, then your feminine attributes are meant to take the lead in that life, and if you are male, male attributes take the lead. A woman may express her feminine energy by nurturing life and using her intuition, beauty, and sensitivity. She may enhance her masculine energy by leadership, mental astuteness, and professionalism. A man may express his masculine energy through accomplishments, wise leadership, and forthrightness. He may draw on his feminine energy when he expresses sensitivity, kindness, and gentle care to those in need.

Even if we're women, we may learn about the qualities of the divine feminine in the male partner of our life or in our sons or our fathers or our brothers, and so forth. We may learn amazing things about the Mother aspect of God. And they may learn many things about the Father aspect of God through us.

While we're still in physical embodiment, our respective

roles, complementing one another, are also like the movement of the tai chi, where even on a daily and hourly basis there are moments when one half of a partnership expresses the feminine qualities to balance the other and one expresses the masculine, and there is an interchange.

The Tai Chi Representing the Masculine-Feminine Polarity of Wholeness.

I'll tell you one more secret about this. When you reach the level of heaven and you are in the tai chi of the white-fire body, it's like the dance of the stars. In the divine exchange of energies, moment by cosmic moment, each half of the whole is at one point male, at one point female. It's like the movement of the waltz, where first one person takes the long step and then the other takes the long step. Just so, two halves of the whole are in the continual dance of the divine polarity.

PART TWO

KARMA
and
RELATIONSHIPS

*All experiences on earth
are to teach us the meaning of love.*

CHAPTER 4

KARMIC RELATIONSHIPS

When we have challenging karma in a relationship, we can experience it as a weight upon our heart and an absence of resolution at the soul level. It's a gnawing condition that troubles our consciousness until it's resolved. Sometimes the relationship seems knotty; we may untangle one aspect only to find another. Simple experiences or interchanges may seem complicated or charged with an edgy energy.

At a conscious or unconscious level, we may have a memory of having been hurt, rejected, or betrayed. Or we may have done these things to another person. Sometimes the more serious the karma, the more intense the experience will be when we first meet someone. Indeed, the impact can be stunning, and this may occur at any time in our life.

It will be stunning because at the subconscious level we are elated that we have found the person with whom we can balance a certain record of karma. Our soul knows that if we do not get through that karma, we cannot go on to the next level of the spiral of life and then on to the world service and creative projects we want to do with the one we love most, even if we haven't met yet.

So we run to greet that one with whom we have karma. We love much because there is much to be forgiven. Our sense of obligation may translate as a need to give of ourselves and to receive, the desire to love and be loved. For the flame of love is the all-consuming fire of God that dissolves the records of nonlove or antilove as we give and take in a relationship.

Our soul knows these things and they are part of why we have come into this life. We have an inner knowing. The soul who is on the homeward path, going home to the Father-Mother God, desires to right the wrongs of the past. She knows that this is the only way to get back to the heavenly place she started from.

LOVE RESOLVES KARMA

When I encounter someone with whom I have difficult and negative interchanges because of intense karma, I have found that God often gives me the gift of intense love. The capacity to love and the release of love seems to happen without my consciously willing it. I feel like the prisoner of this love. My rational mind may be telling me that I should not be loving this person, but my heart loves on.

I have studied this phenomenon in myself, for it is in the laboratory of our own being where we learn the lessons of life. Without my will at all, my heart would become on fire with love for certain people. I did not create this love. I didn't start the fire. God put it in my heart.

If I look back through the years of my life, I can recognize when God placed this kind of love in my heart for someone. Just seeing this person would create within me a heart full of love. I never started the feeling. The love was just there and I observed it, and then I was its prisoner. In cases like these, our karma, seeking resolution, brings us together, and God sends immense love and forgiveness to help us resolve that karma.

It's as if we are drenching the other person in love. When enough love has flowed to balance the karma, all of a sudden the faucet turns off and we no longer have this strong, compelling feeling of love. It's almost unbelievable in contrast to the way we felt before. I've seen this in my own life. I poured out the love, the karma was balanced, and the intensity of that love subsided. It had fulfilled its purpose.

EVERYDAY CHALLENGES

Challenging interactions can be a part of any kind of relationship because any relationship can have difficult karma. And this includes the three types of relationships between couples—twin flames, soul mates, and the karmic relationship. In addition, the degrees of positive or negative karma vary, which may result in anything from a minor, short-term exchange to a long-term involvement.

You may meet key people in your life whom you feel you have known before, and you may have an upbeat positive reaction toward them. You may sense that you have work to do with them, whether through a business, a creative partnership, or another service. This is indicative of a positive karma.

On the other hand, you may have other encounters in which you feel an immediate attraction or recognition but also feel unexplainably ill at ease. It's important to pay attention to this intuitive sense from your soul and other feelings you have. Just because you have known someone or have even been married to that person in a previous life, it doesn't mean you have to get involved. It may be an indication of karma or deep emotional ties, but the relationship can result in reenacting old karmic patterns instead of transcending them. This kind of entanglement can be difficult and can pull you down.

Perhaps you have only a few months' worth of karma to work out with this person. You can render whatever service you feel compelled to give him along life's way, but you do not have to become entangled in a relationship that is detrimental to your spiritual growth.

Therefore you don't want to skip an opportunity to give some gift from your heart to resolve the past when that is what you are called to do. At the same time, you don't want to get entrenched in a situation that causes you to create more karma.

As you move through these relationships, you also realize that there may come a time when the karma is balanced and the relationship is over. You may find that life takes another turn and circumstances change. However the change occurs, when the karma with someone has been balanced, you sense a level of resolution and inner peace. You don't feel the same kind of energy binding you together.

To confirm if you have indeed finally resolved that karma, observe your reactions with this person over time. Are you able to stay centered, sending love and forgiveness in the midst of challenges? Or do you still have strong reactions, possibly resentment or anger, which may indicate areas of nonresolution? You can go into your heart and, through deep prayer, meditation, and soul-searching, attune with God to get the answer.

KARMA *in* MARRIAGES

So aside from twin flames and soul mates, people can have a third kind of marriage—a karmic marriage. It's a marriage in which two individuals are drawn together primarily to balance mutual karma. In a sense, the karmic tie may be the tightest of all. For it is not free; it is binding. Because the karma is not balanced, the couple may experience a lack of harmony. Sometimes they may feel an emptiness, a loneliness, which reveals the inadequacy of a relationship, especially one based solely on karma.

Marriages with much karma can be difficult, but working through it can be an important part of one's process of achieving wholeness. Sometimes these marriages may provide the opportunity for balancing serious karma, such as neglect, violence, or extreme hatred. Very often the only way we can overcome the record of such karma is by the devoted love expressed through the husband-wife relationship.

On the more joyful side, the husband and wife may also gain the good karma of sponsoring and nurturing their children or serving together in some way. And through balancing karma a couple can experience a deepening of their love.

Early in my life I found myself in a relationship in which I eventually discovered that I had some significant past-life karma. While I was in Boston, I met a young man about five years older than I was. He was a law student and a leader in the youth fellowship at our church. The first time I saw him, from a block away, I recognized him; he also recognized me. I knew him, but I did not know him with the powerful impact of love at first sight. I kept on seeing him and I kept on saying to myself, "I know this person. I know this person."

By and by, we became close friends and he eventually asked me to marry him. For some impelling reason that I could not explain, I said yes. I just had the sense and the inner direction that I should do so. But less than a year later, I experienced an undeniable confirmation about my path in life, and it became clear to both of us that our lives were taking us in different directions. So we went our separate ways.

It was heartbreaking for me to end this marriage. I had believed in the relationship and we were good friends and compatible. So in my outer mind I still could not understand why I had married this person to be married only ten months. But my soul knew.

There is an indelible impression in my being of the memory of a past life with him in which I had made serious karma. It was one of the darkest hours of my existence. I had such a burden of remorse for the situation that I had determined to serve this individual until the debt could be paid.

During our marriage in this lifetime, I saw the point where the karma came full circle, right back to the place where it began. I had the opportunity to repeat the initial karmic act all over again, or

I could go beyond it. I made a choice. I stopped in my tracks, and I refused to engage in that karmic momentum. I walked away and I was free.

So sometimes when the karma is resolved, relationships can dissolve. Nevertheless, such relationship situations are not simple, and the best solutions are not always clear. Every situation is unique and, while my situation happened to end in this way, it can be paramount that a couple stay together and work through their karma. When children are involved, it becomes even more important to consider the ramifications of separating. After certain karma is balanced, a couple and a family can experience greater harmony and a deeper love. I have seen this in many relationships. A couple was brought together for karmic reasons, they worked through their karma, and then the relationship evolved into something greater than they had ever imagined.

In karmic marriages the law of God requires that we work through the karma we have with our partner. We don't just walk out on relationships. We determine that whatever the problem is, we are going to resolve it by becoming harmonious and loving and by working with our karmic partner.

When we have mastered our challenges with this person and also served to the level where the karma is balanced, God may change our circumstance. It is important to see this and to not be too quick to move away from those individuals with whom our karma is not balanced. When it is not done in the present, we may have to meet that one again or do some determined spiritual work to resolve that karma.

SMOOTH SAILING *with* POSITIVE KARMA

Sometimes we have relationships or marriages in which we have mostly good karma, and these may provide us with additional positive opportunities. For instance, because of the constructive work for humanity we have done with someone in the past, we may be assigned an even greater responsibility with that person in this life. And because of our good karma, we will be happy and fruitful and have many more accomplishments. We are drawn to such people in joy because we finally have the opportunity to serve with them again.

Positive karma is like the fair wind in our sails that effortlessly propels us forward. Whereas our accumulated negative karma can keep us tied down to the level where we made that karma, our accumulated good karma is like a magnet pulling us up into higher consciousness.

While our negative karma represents our debts to others, our good karma is like having money in our cosmic bank account. It's a reserve we can build on. We can use our good karma—our strengths and positive momentums—to help us overcome and move beyond our negatives.

Good karma can manifest as everything from a supportive circle of family and friends to genius and talent. Our gifts and aptitudes are the seeds of our good karma bearing fruit. The woman who shared the following story clearly had positive karma with her husband.

My husband and I have been married for over fifteen years. We are a good match in that we see life and the world in much the same way, making it easy to make important decisions and to devote ourselves to common goals. We have worked together on environmental issues since before we were married, and there is a feeling of mission and of duty that underlies our reason for being together. There is a strong sense that "We have to do this work and we have to do it together." It has all come naturally and our lives are built around it. It seems that the universe simply made it happen, so we don't even question that this is what we are meant to do. We have a happy and fulfilling marriage, and yet our fulfillment is found mainly through our mutual work and accomplishments together.

LEARNING *from* RELATIONSHIPS

We usually meet people and have relationships with them because our Higher Self wants to convey to us a teaching, which may be a revelation about our own personality. For instance, another person's greatest weakness may mirror our own greatest weakness and we may be drawn to that person so that we can recognize and heal this vulnerability in ourself. Or we may be attracted to people who have developed parts of themselves that we are lacking, those who are opposite from us. So we may feel more complete when we're with such people. This is common, but it is not true wholeness. The more balanced and whole we are, the more we will attract someone who is balanced and whole. If we discern what we are truly seeing in the other person and the teaching we are meant to receive, we will benefit from having seen a reflection of some part of ourself.

Sometimes we may accept a relationship that is less than the highest love and we may wonder why. Perhaps this is because we sell ourselves short. We may feel that we are unworthy of a higher love or even of our twin flame, who is the most wonderful person we can imagine. In selling ourselves short, we sell short the image of the kind of person who might be our partner. Sometimes we even get involved with people who punish us as a way of punishing ourselves. We can see, then, how these kinds of relationships are reflective of our psychology.

For instance, we may be in a relationship that feels confining and limiting, as though a part of our soul simply can't fly and we can't be free. If we feel like this, like we are somehow hemmed in by this relationship, in truth we may be hemmed in by our own psychology and karma. We may even fail somehow in a relationship, whether consciously or unconsciously, just to prove that we are unworthy. We need to have compassion for ourselves, understanding that we do have our psychological vulnerabilities, which probably include the wounds and negative karma from previous lifetimes.

THE INTERPLAY *of* KARMA *and* PSYCHOLOGY

As we experience our relationships, we may recognize that we have many inner strengths, which include a healthy psychology and good karma. We also have weaknesses, or vulnerabilities, which indicate a psychology that could benefit from healing. All of this is intricately intertwined with our karma. At some point in a past life we made karma, which created situations with people that we had to respond to. So we developed ways of reacting, which were repeated, and thus they became patterns.

For example, perhaps in an unguarded moment we got angry and we hurt someone. As a result, we found ourselves in an unavoidable situation with someone who repeatedly became angry with us, so we defended ourselves by becoming passive and pleasing. It worked to some degree when we started, so we kept doing it, especially in close relationships. In this way, our psychology developed out of these karmic circumstances. So our psychology is not merely the result of interpersonal experiences since birth, but it is also the result of karmic situations with certain individuals from other lifetimes.

Working on our psychology helps us to understand ourselves and our relationships. It opens our eyes. We can begin to respond with more insight and less reaction. By combining this with spiritual work, especially the violet flame, we can make great strides in the healing of our psychology. (See Chapter 5.)

WALLS *around the* HEART

In difficult interactions with people, we may unconsciously wall ourselves off. Maybe we were deeply hurt in this life or in a past life and we don't want to open our hearts and be rejected again. Maybe we're angry with others or even with God for the loss of a loved one. Or maybe we feel guilty about our own shortcomings and have convinced ourselves that we don't deserve to be loved. As a result, we build up layers of defenses that we don't even know we have because they are lodged in our unconscious and subconscious minds.

We may retreat into the castle of our heart and position layers of protective walls around it so that no one will get too close to us and we won't get too close to anyone else. We may become more cautious, hiding in the comfort zone of these walls when challenges arise. These defenses keep us insulated from the very thing we want— a relationship in which we can experience a reciprocal love. They also insulate us from the very lessons we need to learn. So how do we heal this?

Although we don't need to know the details of our past lives to successfully work through our karma, it is helpful to self-observe and watch how we react. Whatever is before us is there for a reason; there are no accidents or coincidences in life. Each encounter is a moment when the universe conspires to wake us up and get us back on the high road to a higher love with a greater resolution of karma.

So on the path of balancing karma, sometime, somewhere, we will be on the receiving end of whatever we have put forth. The question is, how will we respond? Will we respond with appreciation or criticism, calmness or anger, generosity or selfishness? Will we be able to truly love? For this is one of the greatest lessons, that no matter what we are faced with, the genuine love of our heart will bring comfort, healing, and resolution.

As Mark Prophet once said, "All experiences on earth are to teach us the meaning of love. All relationships on earth are to teach us the meaning of love. Everything that takes place for the education of the soul is to teach us the meaning of love."

THE INNER DRAMA *of* RELATIONSHIPS

Most of us have been in relationships in which we have experienced strong, unexpected emotional reactions, and it is in our closest relationships that these responses inevitably come out. We may catch ourselves in a mood that we can hardly believe is native to us. We may suddenly become angry. We may notice we have become terribly jealous. We may feel irritated with someone.

While these reactions can originate from situations in our current lives, they can also signal the possibility of an unresolved issue from a past life. Every time we get a glimpse of one of these patterns, we can take notice and recognize it. In this way, we are not suppressing it and pushing it back into our subconscious. Rather, we have identified it and then we can make a conscious effort to understand and transform it, as the woman in the following story did.

> *Throughout my marriage, I have had experiences that I can only describe as "a karmic pocket," a clue to a past-life karma. On the surface the situation is an everyday one, yet my internal world is in somersaults, with my emotions reactive and volatile. For example, some years ago there was a mild illness in the household and my family was somewhat worn out. There was a moment during one of those busy family times when I was cooking dinner when a small request from my husband triggered strong resentment in me. Because of the unexpected intensity, I felt that it was a karmic pocket and I kept quiet so I could become calmer. Awhile later when I was more settled, I realized that with everyone being sick our emotional reserves were low. I sensed that my unexpected resentment harkened back to a past life. I had a vague memory of a time when I was also vulnerable, even to the point of feeling terrified and angry for being left alone to fend for myself.*
>
> *Karmic pockets sometimes take longer to work through, even weeks, after an unexpected argument or eruption of emotions. My husband and I have found that these times call for honest talks and inner work. And we also focus on doing fun things together to nourish our love, such as date nights, playing a game, or hiking in the mountains.*

In addition to past-life issues, often such strong responses are based on earlier events in our current life. As we were growing up, we absorbed our childhood experiences with parents and others who were important to us. These became part of our internal makeup and contributed to an inner world that plays a key part in the drama of our relationships.

As explained earlier, the soul is impressionable. She is naturally accepting and open, absorbing from those around her without having positive or negative judgments about right and wrong. In this innocent, vulnerable state, she looks up to the authority figures in her life, which usually begin with her father and mother as representatives of the Father-Mother God, and she takes in what they send out.

Whatever the soul absorbs becomes part of her inner world, part of her psychology. We can see the soul as a child who lives inside of us, our "inner child." Since we have had many positive and negative experiences, we carry within us a loved, healthy inner child as well as an unloved, wounded inner child.

If we were cherished and appreciated when we were growing up, an inner child who feels loved, a healthy inner child, was formed. This is the part of us that is enthusiastic, creative, intuitive, childlike, innocent, and trusting. If we were neglected, abused, or dismissed, an inner child who feels unloved, a wounded inner child, was formed. The wounded inner child internalizes these negative experiences and has a fragile sense of self-worth.

To protect ourself from more pain, we develop certain habits of thinking, feeling, and acting, which are usually more detrimental than helpful. Then when we get into relationships, we react out of these habits. And just about all of us do this to some degree. This is how our inner world affects our relationships.

For example, in order to avoid conflict, we may accommodate another person's bad habits or we may not draw necessary boundaries. To keep people from getting too close, we may dominate or criticize them. To make sure that we are liked, we may put someone on a pedestal and defer to that person excessively. So inner pain can show up in many different ways.

Thus the soul is trying to help and protect herself, yet this usually does not result in the best outcome. When we understand ourselves and why and how we do these things, we can heal from the inner pain and interact differently, as the young woman in the following story realized.

In my early twenties I dated an older man who I believed was the love of my life. We played musical instruments together, sharing exciting and rather dramatic experiences. I minimized his flirting and drug habits and convinced myself that it was all okay in order to maintain a so-called peaceful relationship. But through these compromises, I was getting further and further away from my true self.

I noticed that when I was alone I felt vaguely depressed. Although I wasn't conscious of it at the time, I now know that I wasn't being energized by my inner being but rather entangled in karma. My self-respect was being whittled away. Then one day the inevitable happened. He broke up with me and it was devastating.

After much soul-searching, I realized that I had magnetized this relationship because of a lack of self-worth. In college, I was confused and lacked confidence. I was also vulnerable because of the strong attraction and obvious karma I had with this man. And so, I made this man utterly "perfect" so that I didn't have to face my inner pain. And in the process I gave away so much of my true self.

This experience was a huge wake-up call. It propelled me on a deep spiritual search to heal because I didn't want to repeat this type of relationship.

HEALING *the* SOUL

An essential part of finding wholeness in our relationships is healing our inner child. It's easy to react to others according to the habits we have developed, even when we're with those with whom we want to have a good relationship. Our energy tends to flow automatically into those old habit patterns. But when we begin to heal the wounded inner child, that same energy is liberated, and then it can flow the way that we want it to, into loving and supportive interactions and relationships.

How do we do this? Our inner child needs a helper, and we do have one. It is the loving inner adult, who is patterned after our Higher Self. The loving inner adult contains the loving messages that we have taken in from parents and others. It is the part of us that is the wise and loving mother and father to our inner child. However, we also have an unloving inner adult, who can, for example, criticize or indulge us. And most of us have elements of both.[1]

We learn how to treat ourselves and others from the way that our parents treated us. If our parents were loving, then we would tend to treat our inner child and others in a loving, respectful manner. But if we had dismissive parents, for example, we may ignore the needs of our inner child and lack sensitivity to the needs of others.

When we enter relationships, it's not unusual for us to gravitate toward those who are similar to our parents. Unconsciously, we are re-creating our relationship with our parents so that we can try to heal it. We often have areas of nonresolution with them. For when we are born, the first karma we meet is with our parents, and this can be our most challenging karma as well as a very positive karma.

So sometimes our reactions in our adult relationships are related more to feelings from experiences with our parents than from the person we are with. This is what happened to the following couple during a moment of stress in their daily family life.

My husband and I recently had an argument about what our children are allowed to watch on TV. When an upsetting scene came across the screen, I covered the eyes of our young child and shouted, "Turn it off!" I was so alarmed and upset that my usual calm voice became loud and aggressive. This caused a deep reaction in my husband. Instead of agreeing with me and turning the TV off, he was upset because I yelled at him, making me even more upset.

He later explained that his knee-jerk reaction was triggered by the hurt he still felt from being yelled at as a child. Once I realized this, I could understand why he reacted out of character to his usual reasonable approach. I explained to him that I can get very upset when I don't feel heard or understood, an effect from my own childhood. When we both realized the origin of our reactions, we saw that they had more to do with our childhood experiences with our parents than with one another. We gained a greater compassion for each other, and so in the end the incident brought us closer.

Little by little as we strive to forgive ourselves, forgive others, seek resolution, and work through our emotions, portions of our inner child and inner adult are drawing nearer to our Higher Self. Through the loving heart of our Higher Self, our inner child is healed step-by-step. We pay attention to this child, we listen, and we love her with understanding, comfort, and patience as she is healing on the path to becoming whole. To assist us in our healing, we can ask our Higher Self to direct us to anything else we might need, such as a specific book, therapy, or some other source of support.[2]

As we strive to help our inner child bond with our inner loving adult, we are building the foundation for the full and final bonding of our soul with our Higher Self. And the great gift and blessing is this: Any portion of our inner child and inner adult that has become whole through being loved is already one with our Higher Self.

With determination and a desire for change, we can begin to take apart the components of the problem we are working through. We can name the experience. We can write it down on paper, and as we write it, we may get a broader perspective. We can pray to God to help us surrender and transform painful experiences with parents and others. In this way we can re-create ourselves day-by-day. At the same time, our Higher Self can stand guard to help our soul heal and find resolution. And all along the way, God sees us immaculately, in our divine wholeness. No matter what we are working through, we can affirm the truth: "I AM loved by my Father-Mother God."

I AM LIGHT!

In the midst of daily life, when your soul is in need of remembering her divine identity, you can give the decree "I AM Light!" As you give this decree, meditate upon your soul's union with your Higher Self, God Presence, and twin flame. Imagine that you are light. See the white-fire radiance infilling and surrounding you and your loved ones. As various thoughts and feelings arise, you can release them into this light. If you have a difficult time visualizing, as some people do, find a picture of a beautiful waterfall and keep it before you as you give this decree. See a great waterfall of light sweeping through any difficulties in your psychology and in your relationships.

You can give this mantra three times, nine times, or as many times as you like. Watch to see how your circumstances can change and how you can be blessed by the light.

> **I AM light, glowing light,**
> **Radiating light, intensified light.**
> **God consumes my darkness,**
> **Transmuting it into light.**

This day I AM a focus of the central sun.
Flowing through me is a crystal river,
A living fountain of light
That can never be qualified
By human thought and feeling.
I AM an outpost of the Divine.
Such darkness as has used me is swallowed up
By the mighty river of light which I AM!

I AM, I AM, I AM light;
I live, I live, I live in light.
I AM light's fullest dimension;
I AM light's purest intention.
I AM light, light, light
Flooding the world everywhere I move,
Blessing, strengthening, and conveying
The purpose of the kingdom of heaven.

MAKING *a* PLACE *for* YOUR AUTHENTIC SELF

Mark once said, "Be love simply, purely, and wholly. Do what comes naturally, not that which is contrived. Do what your heart tells you to do. Help one another. Forgive one another, as you ask God for forgiveness."

Learning how to act naturally, authentically, and not in a contrived way can sometimes be the hardest part of relationships. I remember that one of the most important lessons I learned when I was in high school and college was how to be true to myself in relationships. Sometimes someone would ask me out and I would know that he didn't perceive me for who I truly was but rather for who he wanted me to be.

At times we may find ourselves in such a situation and we may act out a part in order to be liked by certain people. If we are feeling insecure or perhaps unaccepted, we may think, "If I don't dress like these people, look like them, talk like them, act like them, and do the things they do, they will never love me."

So we may become actors on the stage of life. And if we play a role, perhaps to be accepted or approved of, then we may lose a part of ourselves, and this can be painful. Sometimes people even get married as part of acting out a role or establishing themselves in society. If you ever find yourself trapped in such a situation and you're trying to find the point of reality, it may be necessary to separate yourself out for a while in order to gain a stronger sense of self.

We may even prefer to be alone for a time rather than to change our appearance and our personality for the sake of others. To be true to ourselves, to be authentic, we may be, for a while, a solitary one—one who knows who he is and is willing to wait to become part of a greater reality—because we are looking for that higher love. The man in the following story realized just in time that he had been acting out a role without even being aware of it.

I met someone with whom I felt a deep and special connection, unlike anything I had ever felt with anyone else. But I still kept dating girls of my own faith because I knew that my parents would not approve of this girl since her beliefs were not the same. Meanwhile, I was studying to be a doctor, something I had literally been told that I would be since I was a child. I successfully got into a top medical school, and then one day I realized that I had no true passion for medicine. At the same time, I was about to be engaged to a genuinely nice person of my own faith whom I did not really love. Through soul-searching and reflection, I finally discovered that I had spent most of my life trying to fulfill my parents' dreams and I had never figured out who I was and what I wanted to be. I had been acting out a part without realizing it.

WHOLESOME FRIENDSHIPS *and* POSITIVE KARMA

When we are true to ourselves, we can attract those who appreciate us for who we really are. Such appreciation, when it is reciprocal, is the foundation for a true friendship at any age. For teens and young adults, relationships can be especially difficult and sometimes karma-making. During this time, being authentic and true to ourselves with peers is perhaps one of the greatest challenges.

In these years we're naturally building our identity and determining how and where we fit into the groups in our life—at school, in a job, in sports, and in other activities. At the same time, we're experiencing sexual energies and figuring out how we're going to deal with these energies in ourselves as well as in our relationships. Even in the best of friendships, sexual attractions and energies can occur, but they can be dealt with in healthy, balanced, and effective ways. (See Chapter 7.)

In contrast, when a strong sexual component is the basis of a relationship, this can become the focus, overshadowing the development of other aspects of a healthy relationship. Even without the sexual involvement, a relationship can revolve too much around superficial personalities, which can lead to petty conflicts. All of these entanglements can create and compound artificial, karma-making relationships. After experiencing the disappointments of such relationships, the young woman in the following story discovered a vital key to finding a higher love.

When I've been in relationships, I've sometimes felt that I was losing my individuality. So at some point I realized that I had to take time to learn who I really am. It wasn't until I was completely clear of infatuations, crushes, or misconceived love that I could look deeply inside myself and discover who I am at my very core.

Being single has been one of the most difficult but important things I've ever done. And it has been a key to my happiness. I feel like it will also contribute to a truly happy relationship in the future. How can I expect a relationship to make me happy if I can't be happy on my own?

I've discovered so much power in finding my own joy. I know that since this is now inside me, no one can take it away. I am no longer relying on another person to fulfill all of my needs and to make me happy because I've already done that on my own. Now that these needs are filled within myself, I feel like I can be much more open to a vibrant, healthy, and fulfilling relationship.

Taking your time in being single can include establishing and enjoying solid friendships, and it is one of the most helpful ways to navigate through the young adult years. Doing group activities together with friends rather than having the pressure of one-on-one male-female relationships can strengthen these friendships.

The expression of love in wholesome and creative ways is one of the most important parts of a real friendship. These can include community service or other activities like sports, music, or drama, perhaps getting involved in a local theater group. This type of friendship may or may not become a serious or romantic relationship. It may be short-lived or it may be long-lasting. In any case, the support and encouragement for each one's true identity is the foundation for any strong relationship you may have in the future.

The words of Kahlil Gibran reflect the spirit of this kind of friendship:

When your friend speaks his mind you fear not the "nay" in your
     own mind, nor do you withhold the "ay."
And when he is silent our heart ceases not to listen to his heart;
For without words, in friendship, all thoughts, all desires, all expec-
     tations are born and shared, with joy that is unclaimed.
When you part from your friend, you grieve not;

For that which you love most in him may be clearer in his absence,
  as the mountain to the climber is clearer from the plain.
And let there be no purpose in friendship save the deepening of the
  spirit.
For love that seeks aught but the disclosure of its own mystery is
  not love but a net cast forth: and only the unprofitable is caught.

And let your best be for your friend.
If he must know the ebb of your tide, let him know its flood also.
For what is your friend that you should seek him with hours to kill?
Seek him always with hours to live.
For it is his to fill your need, but not your emptiness.
And in the sweetness of friendship let there be laughter, and sharing
  of pleasures.
For in the dew of little things the heart finds its morning and is
  refreshed.[3]

CHAPTER 5

HEALING *and* TRANSFORMING
RELATIONSHIPS

One way to change the human patterns in our relationships is to have a wider perspective and a change of heart. In the inevitable challenges of relationships, we may have a limited concept about others. Having a perspective from the heart broadens our viewpoint and helps us to accept people as they are, to allow them to be who they are, and to try to learn from everyone we meet.

We will have all kinds of relationships with people who may not fit the mold of what we want or expect, but they may have something precious inside of them—a gift, an idea, a unique understanding. With an open mind and heart, we can invite others to share what is inside of them, and chances are that they can't wait to do so. And chances are that we can discover something new by listening to them.

From a perspective of higher love, we can look beyond outer appearances to the inner essence. What is the inner essence of yourself? What makes you special? What makes you full of joy, love, and happiness? What enables you to give to others? We can see others from this same standpoint, a perspective that we can cultivate.

A young woman I gave counsel to had this kind of change in outlook about her quiet husband.

When I first met my husband, I thought he was the sweetest man in the world. By and by we got married and, as is often the case with newlyweds, I realized that he wasn't perfect. Being a rather verbose female, I assumed that somehow he would be just as communicative as my equally verbose girlfriends. He was considerate, kind, funny, and hardworking. But he didn't talk a lot, and I worried about this.

One day Mrs. Prophet asked me how married life was. I paused, not wanting to seem ungrateful, and then I said in a forlorn voice, "Well, he doesn't talk very much." She waited a moment and then she said, "He communicates. He's a real heart person. He communicates with his heart."

I told my husband what she said. Sometime later we were at home sitting quietly next to each other on the couch, not saying very much. And he said to me very softly, "Can you hear me? I'm speaking to you." I could almost hear his heart beating in tones of love. I only needed to listen.

Many years have passed. My husband talks much more now, but it doesn't even matter. For I've learned to listen, and I know now that I was right in the very beginning about his sterling sweet heart.

THE LIGHT *of* COMPASSION

In relationships built on mutual compassion, both people have room to be who they are. Each one respects the needs of the other, and they help one another to blossom. They honor each other's personal relationship to God and striving for God. This is a truly loving relationship that energizes both people and fosters the greatest growth.

Compassion is the kind of love that lifts and ennobles others. It is a love that goads them to reach their full potential. And so this love, this compassion, will not leave others where it finds them. Rather, it is a love that will support and encourage them in their relationship with the truest and best part of themselves, with their Higher Self, and with their God.

Many of the great saints and holy men and women have understood and demonstrated the significance of this kind of love. A disciple of the Buddha once asked his teacher if it would be true to say that a part of their training is for the development of love and compassion. The teacher replied that no, it would not be true to say this; it would be true to say that the *whole* of their training is for the development of love and compassion.

To plumb the depths of such compassion, we dip into the fire of our heart to the place of our deepest, purest love.

The Compassionate Buddha

We can imagine this place as a fiery furnace, and from there the flame of our heart extends to enfold the one who needs that love. Thus, from our heart we send a depth of love and understanding.

This pure love of our hearts can translate to someone else as comfort. When our loved ones feel our comfort, they can be at ease. Not fearing judgment, their soul may experience healing and release a heavy burden. We might be amazed at how much we can help, how many problems can be healed, how much of a past karmic record can be erased. Our presence, our voice, our comfort, our love, our companionship can help dissolve it. And we can watch how that one will take flight and soar, barely realizing that such a record has been resolved. Our relationships will take on a new and higher love.

Simple devotions can help us to broaden our perspective and cultivate our hearts. For instance, you can take just a little time each day to go within your heart and feel the presence of God, recognizing his presence in all things, and you can say with gratitude, "O God, you are so magnificent!"

One aspect of compassion is softness of heart. Softness is a nurturing, giving attitude. It responds from a position of centeredness in the heart. It doesn't react to another's anger or emotions with more of the same. Rather, it is a receptive mode whereby unnatural, forceful human actions give way to the natural love of the heart.

Softness is strength, the ultimate strength. It is the opposite of brittleness, rigidity, or resistance. Rigidity and resistance to change, including changes in relationships, can make us brittle. And, as we know, brittle things can easily break. Softness is a gentle way of dealing with a situation that doesn't degrade the other person but shows him that we have only his best interest at heart.

Often people are a little rough around the edges. They have a unique beauty inside of them that they may not yet be showing. They're still growing into the fullness of their best self. With this understanding, we can care for each one as a tender flower. And then we may find that the gentle approach, while not being sympathetic, uplifts the very one who has the most challenges and, perhaps, who challenges us the most. In the following story, the flow of genuine compassion softened this man's heart.

A few years ago while I was swimming in the ocean, I was praying about a difficult situation in my marriage. My wife and I kept repeating the same arguments about work and schedules. I felt pushed by her, and she would get frustrated and tell me what I was doing wrong (or at least that's what I heard). We both got prickly and defensive. So as I was swimming I suddenly remembered the adage my parents taught me, "Walk in the other person's shoes for a time." And so I let the water wash through my frustration and I asked God to let me experience what she was experiencing, to really feel and be "in her shoes." The change was subtle, yet remarkable. I noticed that the next time this issue came up, I was able to listen to her with a lot more patience, and my heart felt more open. In times of stress, I remember this simple wisdom from my parents. It has truly been pivotal for our marriage.

THE DAMPER *of* SYMPATHY

Unlike compassion, sympathy identifies with the human self of another. It disposes others to indulge in their weaknesses and to feel sorry for themselves. It encourages what could be called a horizontal relationship with others rather than the vertical relationship of looking to, and reaching for, one's Higher Self. It may provide a temporary relief or partial comfort, but ultimately it may bring a downward feeling. It de-energizes.

Sometimes people create a sympathetic pull through self-pity. This can evoke in us feelings of obligation, even intimidation. They may convey the message "You owe it to me to take care of me, to help me, to give me your light, your money, your support, your time and space because I can't do it for myself since I'm in such a merciless plight." It's a pull, even a magnetism, that is easy to get caught up in when we genuinely care for others and want to assist them. But if we are vigilant and recognize this, we can choose to respond with true compassion, which sometimes may be to allow others to face and work through their own struggles.

In a sympathetic relationship, one or both people may feel that they can't fully be themselves. For they have a relationship in which they look outward to another for direction instead of inward. These relationships are often disappointing because each one is looking to the other for what ultimately can only come from their relationship with their Higher Self and with God.

THE VIOLET FLAME

Another way to expand love in our hearts and in our relationships is through a unique spiritual energy called the violet fire, or violet flame. (See Plate 5.) You may remember seeing this vivid color of light through a crystal or a prism. If you've looked closely, perhaps you've noticed how a ray of sunlight, when passed through a prism, will separate into a myriad array of colors.

Isaac Newton, the great physicist and mathematician, observed that the light ray will separate into the seven colors of the rainbow: red, orange, yellow, green, blue, indigo, and violet. This visible light is only a tiny portion of an electromagnetic spectrum of varying frequencies, or wavelengths, which include radio waves, micro-waves, infrared radiation, ultraviolet radiation, X-rays, gamma rays, and cosmic rays.

Today scientists know of about sixty to seventy octaves of light. Violet, with the shortest wavelength, has the highest frequency in the visible spectrum and is at the point of transition to the next octave of light. At the same time, out of all the colors of the visible spectrum the violet light is the closest in vibration to matter, to earth substance. When the dense substance of the physical plane contacts the violet flame, it is transformed, or transmuted.[1]

ALCHEMICAL TRANSFORMATION

Transmutation means "to alter in form, appearance, or nature, especially to change something into a higher form." This term was used by alchemists of old who attempted to transmute base metals into gold, separating the "subtle" from the "gross" by means of heat.

These alchemists did not reveal what they were truly seeking, which was far more than the transformation of metals. They wanted to contact the nexus of the flow where Spirit became matter and matter became Spirit, which is the point of the violet flame. They were, in fact, pursuing the soul's union with the Higher Self. These alchemists were mystics who were concerned with the acceleration of consciousness and the transformation of the soul.

For both ancient and medieval alchemists, the real purpose of alchemical transmutation was spiritual transformation and the attainment of eternal life. And this is what the violet flame can give you—the action of transformation and rejuvenation. It consumes the elements of our karma and everything that is not of our ultimate reality into the golden nature of our divine self.

THE VIOLET FLAME *in* YOUR LIFE *and* RELATIONSHIPS

The action of the violet flame can bring healing to our physical body as well as our psychology. It can enhance the action of forgiveness. It can help us get through unresolved experiences with people who have wronged us or whom we have wronged.

The violet flame is the joie de vivre that can bring joy and upliftment. It helps to free our souls. It is the energy of mercy, freedom, and transmutation. The violet flame can bring miracles into our life.

How do you get the violet flame to do these things for you and your relationships? You can call forth this light with violet-flame mantras and decrees. As you do, visualize this flame erasing the records of past trials and testings. You can start this process by giving the following simple violet-flame mantra, repeating it as many times as you would like.

I AM a being of violet fire!
I AM the purity God desires!

The violet flame can clear old karmic hurts and blocks to love and loving relationships. Based on our past, these are different for each of us, and they can manifest as anything from fear, anger, irritation, depression, and selfishness to hardness of heart. Whatever these challenges are for you, the violet flame can work to clear them. When the woman in the following story tried it out, she was happily surprised.

I have found that my husband often gets very emotional when I don't even know what he is upset about. This can be disheartening and disturbing. Sometimes when this happens, I simply step away for a few minutes and focus on the following mantra:

My husband is a being of violet fire!
My husband is the purity God desires!

I AM a being of violet fire!
I AM the purity God desires!

Time and time again, I have found that the energy shifts immediately. My husband lets go of the feelings he was having, he becomes forgiving, and he almost completely forgets about whatever had upset him. The violet flame dissolves the issues! Sometimes I just give the mantra for a few minutes, but the benefits are still amazing!

As you give the following mantra or any violet-flame decree, you can visualize the violet flame burning in your heart and surrounding your heart. Feel the love in your heart expand and extend to those you love and to those with whom you want resolution and healing.

You can increase the action of the violet flame through your visualization and the fervor of your call. As you give the following mantra, imagine the violet light slowly expanding and becoming so intense that you can't even see through it.

Violet fire, thou love divine,
Blaze within this heart of mine!
Thou art mercy forever true,
Keep me always in tune with you.

THE FREEDOM *of* FORGIVENESS

Most people have a natural desire for harmony within themselves as well as in their relationships. A key to achieving harmony in our own psyche as well as in our interactions with others is through mercy and forgiveness—mercy whereby we forgive ourself, mercy whereby we forgive others.

To receive God's forgiveness, we begin by forgiving ourselves. We can forgive ourselves for being human and for making mistakes. All of us are human, and we've all done things we're not proud of. All of us have had to go through our experiences in the best way we knew how at the time. Sometimes it wasn't the most perfect way, but that is the process of learning—experiencing, going through trial and error, and then finally coming out on top.

We should never condemn ourselves for our shortcomings and mistakes, but we can resolve to do better next time. If we condemn ourselves even a little, it's like poking a hole in a water bottle. The water slowly but surely leaks out. No matter how much water we put in the bottle, it will not stay full. That's what happens to our energy when we allow anything or anyone, including ourselves, to condemn us so that we feel we are not worthy of God's love. Our soul *is* worthy. She is worthy of God's love and forgiveness.

So with profound mercy, forgive yourself for the errors and karma of this and previous lifetimes, whether you remember them or not. If you truly forgive yourself, you establish a magnet of forgiveness in your heart, which draws down God's forgiveness. Accepting God's forgiveness is the foundation for resolution. When you receive forgiveness, something is lifted, some percentage of the weight of karma, the burden of the act itself. Therefore forgiveness is an important part of balancing karma.

We can look at the people we are tied to today. We can look at our situation with our job, our family, and everything that affects us. Most of us have difficult people in our lives. Sometimes we can't seem to resolve issues with them or to disentangle ourselves. Often it's because we've never forgiven old hurts and old wrongs. This nonforgiveness binds us so tightly to people that we may feel like we can never rise above the arguments and the problems. But in order to expand love, we need to let go of these things.

We need to forgive and forget and move on. We can bless life and be free. The greatest liberation I have achieved in this life is the ability to forgive all people profoundly, deeply, and with the totality of my being.

HEALING RELATIONSHIPS *with* FORGIVENESS

Forgiveness is a two-step process. We pray for divine mercy and forgive the soul of the one who committed the wrongdoing, and we also ask God to forgive that soul. When a person does something that hurts another, he is not acting from his Real Self but from what can be called his not-self. Next we pray for divine justice for the not-self and for the person to be free from it. Although we truly forgive the soul, we do not accept the wrong deed or the consciousness behind it. This can be a great liberation, especially when we want to forgive a soul but their action was indeed grievous. We forgive the soul but not the deed. Engaging in this process can help us forgive even those whom we have the hardest time forgiving.

We also ask God to give the soul the opportunity to make amends for her deeds and to strengthen herself so she can resist the urge to do wrong when it knocks again at her door. We usually don't know the cause behind another person's actions. Even if we think we know, there may be underlying issues that we are not aware of. Therefore we don't need to judge or punish. Rather, beyond the personality and the deed, we can perceive the soul and offer forgiveness and compassion. And this may just be the gift that not only frees us but also frees that soul.

Forgiveness doesn't always happen all at once; it usually happens in increments. Each night as we lay our bodies down to sleep, it's the end of a cycle and we have a chance to forgive. It's our time to let go of all discord and problems and to forgive every part of life. We want to turn the page of the day and pray for the interactions of the day to be resolved.

So we practice forgiveness every day, every night. And as we do, we are taking firm steps toward our goal. For little by little as we work through our emotions, forgive ourselves, forgive others, and come to resolution, portions of ourselves are daily becoming part of our Higher Self, our Real Self.

The forgiving heart is the liberated heart. When we extend mercy from our heart and we follow it with lots of violet flame, we can experience a sense of liberation. We can send blessings and love and light. And if the other person harbors anger and resentment, that is something for him to work through. We just have to know that our forgiveness is absolute, total, true, and profound, and then we can truly say, "I have forgiven."

A FORGIVENESS MEDITATION

We can practice forgiveness by sending violet flame into the cause, effect, record, and memory of every negative interchange we have ever had and its harmful effect upon us and the other person. We can ask for everyone who was affected by the situation to also be delivered by violet-flame transmutation.

Think of an instance when someone has wronged or hurt you. If it was a painful situation, remember that you can forgive that person's soul. Ask God to work with that soul and to show you how to forgive, including whether you need to take any other positive action. To assist with the process of forgiveness, try using the following meditation and affirmation.

Imagine yourself standing under a gentle, violet-colored waterfall that washes away any sense of guilt or blame, shame or condemnation. Let the soothing water of forgiveness flow in, through, and around you, giving your soul a sense of peace.

Next, repeat the following affirmation to draw down the violet-flame action of mercy and forgiveness. See your heart becoming a magnet for forgiveness.

> **I AM a being of violet fire!**
> **I AM the purity God desires!**

Now imagine a sphere of violet light surrounding those whom you want to forgive, dissolving all negativity and filling their souls with the light of forgiveness. Then repeat the following affirmation for each one of them, inserting his or her name in the blank:

> **_____ is a being of violet fire!**
> **_____ is the purity God desires!**

You can also give the following decree for forgiveness as you visualize spheres of violet flame carried on wings of light and being delivered to all whom you forgive or who need to forgive you:

> **I AM forgiveness acting here,**
> **Casting out all doubt and fear,**
> **Setting men forever free**
> **With wings of cosmic victory.**
>
> **I AM calling in full power**
> **For forgiveness every hour;**
> **To all life in every place**
> **I flood forth forgiving grace.**

TRANSMUTING PAST BURDENS

It is never too early or too late to call forth the violet flame for your relationships. The violet flame can transmute burdens in our current and recent relationships and it can also retroactively transmute karmic records and memories from past lives. So we can apply the violet flame to present matters of the heart and rough spots in our relationships. These could be, for instance, the burden of losing a friend or a loved one or the burden of watching someone close to us go through hard times.

At some time, you may find yourself recalling glimpses of past lives, perhaps after you have been giving the violet flame for a while. You may have a dream or an intuition about your soul or about close relationships in ages long past. Or you may just have an impression of a particular time or place. Such past-life records and memories are like computer files in the subconscious mind. If you become aware of these memories, you don't need to suppress them. Instead, focus your attention on the light in your heart and imagine the experience saturated with the violet flame until the image disappears from before your inner sight. Then let go of the memory and see a bright, white sun replacing the image in your mind's eye.

Along with the givingness of self and the giving of love and service, karma can be cleared away by the scrubbing action of the violet flame. You can repeat the following short decree to help clean out the karma between yourself and others. It can also anchor in you the light of your Higher Self.

> **Violet fire blazing,**
> **Violet fire blazing,**
> **Violet fire blazing,**
> **God's own light is raising, raising, raising**
> **All my thoughts, consciousness, too,**
> **To the plane of my Presence, who**
> **In God's name releases all**
> **Wisdom and balance for which I call.**

JOY *and* LAUGHTER

You can also do simple things every day to increase the energy of the violet flame in your life and your relationships. For example, since joy is a quality of the violet flame, you can practice being joyful.

Joy is the bubbling essence of God's love expressed in your life. It is magnetic and contagious. When we have the simplicity of joy in our relationships, it brings peace and comfort to those we love. They become more joyous and their life seems lighter. It's easier for us to feel the love in our hearts when we share joy with someone else. So joy keeps the love flowing from one heart to another.

My husband Mark demonstrated joy like no one else I've ever known. He conveyed the miracle of joy by his example and in his teaching to us:

> Laugh a little bit over some of the silly circumstances that happen.... And if you can learn to laugh at yourself, well then you've really got something!
>
> Then what have we got? It's partly a matter of what we have gotten rid of. When we laugh at ourselves and don't take ourselves too seriously, we're removing the mask of the human ego and putting our Higher Self in its place. And this is partly why, deep in their hearts, people do like to laugh at themselves. And this too is contagious!
>
> So learn to laugh at yourself and your foibles, and enjoy life! Don't forget to play hard too! And love—love yourself and be grateful for the unique facet of God that you are.

You can also give the following violet-flame mantra to increase joy and bring happiness into your life and relationships.

> **Come, violet fire!**
> **Descend into my form!**
> **Thy consecrated purity,**
> **Bringing cosmic ecstasy**
> **Making me to be like thee—**
> **Adorn my being now!**

The joyful three-quarter time of waltz music is the same rhythm as your heartbeat and carries the energy and vibration of the violet flame. You can whistle the violet flame or sing it. You can jump and dance to it or make games out of it. You can come up with all kinds of fun and innovative ways to bring the violet flame into your relationships and every area of your life. Children, and your inner child, love the violet flame![2]

QUESTIONS & ANSWERS
with Elizabeth Clare Prophet on

Karma and Relationships

LOVE *and* FORGIVENESS

Q: How can I love people unconditionally?

A: You cannot love naughty deeds in people, and God doesn't expect you to. But you can love the soul. You can love the person and you can love their God Presence. And the more off-track the person becomes, the more your love ascends and is on fire for the Higher Self of that person to be magnetized back to him so that his outer self will reflect it.

You could have a present awareness of the potential of the individual to become who he or she really is. You love that potential, and you love the God that loved this person and said, "I've sent you forth to become myself. I've given you the opportunity to live."

When God put us on the earth, he allowed for the possibility that we would make mistakes and that we would not become God-free, we would not become part of him as individuals, if we didn't go through the process of learning by trial and error.

So when you realize God's unconditional love for each individual in giving him free will and sending him forth with that will, you realize that you must love as God loves.

In my prayers to God concerning my love for someone who might have been difficult to love, I have allowed my consciousness to go to God because I wanted to get a perspective on how

God was loving this individual. And many times my love has increased for that person.

Unconditional love is the unconditional love of the right of the individual to become who he is. It is the love which allows him to pass through that process without our heckling, badgering, henpecking, criticizing, or becoming irritated.

Now, let's say that the person you love does something you don't like. You may have an intense love for that person, and when it is a love that comes from your Higher Self, it immediately registers within you what is not right. So then you know that you cannot just stand by and let the universe and yourself be trampled upon by that negative energy. So quietly but firmly you have to make the statement: "This is not something I can join you in. This is not something I can go along with, and you cannot do this in my presence." And then you hope and pray that this person can move through the problem.

And this is why in a marriage you should be equally yoked. You should be able to trust that a person will not involve you in negatives patterns that would be totally unacceptable to you. You would not plight your troth with such a person, because you would not take on that energy. And the more you love God, the more you say, "If there is not a certain respect for the dignity of the Higher Self within both of us, this relationship will afford no future."

But if your absence of unconditional love is a point of personal pride, absence of trust, or absence of commitment to the relationship, then you have to realize that this may be your own selfishness and fear. It is trust that makes a relationship work and by which you are bound together. Trust is the covenant and contract of marriage. And if that trust is broken because whenever the other person does something you don't like, you state your objections and shut down, then you're not ready for such a contract. You may love, but you may not be ready to shoulder the burdens of a marriage relationship. So you may need to grow more before you make such a commitment.

Of course if people break your trust, especially repeatedly, it is understandable if you lose your trust in them. In that case, they need to strive to merit your trust.

KARMIC ENTANGLEMENTS

Q: **What do I do if I created karma in a past relationship and want to make sure it's resolved?**

A: If a relationship is over, it's over for a reason. It came to its logical conclusion. Everything that could be derived from it was derived. But sometimes there's a certain nostalgia because when we move forward and progress in life, we somehow imagine the person we once knew as now having the same relationship to us as he did when we were together and it was good. But of course that couldn't happen in the present unless that person had made the same progress as we have.

And most often you find that when you go back, for instance, to your hometown, people haven't changed. You're the one who has changed.

If your relationship with the person was in the far past and you don't have any reason to communicate and it's over and done with, you can pray that he finds what he needs in life.

Q: **Under what circumstances do you recommend breaking up with someone?**

A: The time to break up is the point at which you realize that there is nothing served by the relationship. The relationship is not contributing to a spiritual or even a positive consciousness in the two individuals involved. It is not unlocking the best creative forces in each of the people, and one person or the other may be encroaching on the other's reason for being or their growth.

I personally would not allow anyone to encroach upon my freedom to be who I am. I don't mind being flexible, pliable, stepping aside. I am not adverse to self-effacement in order that another one may increase. But there comes a point when some people manage to eclipse the sun of your own spiritual presence, even to the point of affecting your ability to function. I would not allow that, and that is my free will, which I consider to be essential.

Another reason for a breakup would be when the relationship produces any negative quality or you notice in yourself or in the other person an increasing lowering of the joy of life. You may sometimes get despondent or depressed. This may be because something within one or both of you is detrimental to the unfoldment and realization of your partner's potential to be the highest and best part of himself.

You might also break up with someone because you recognize that the purpose of the relationship has already been fulfilled. Something has been gained, both parties have benefited, and there no longer seems to be a benefit or mutual interest.

Q: How do you know when your karma in a certain relationship is completed?

A: A relationship can come to a resolution. It can run the whole gamut—from an intense love relationship to intense argumentation, perhaps an intense love-hate relationship—and then you can come to a point of peace and a point of mutual giving and service to one another. Or you can come to the place where the relationship doesn't seem to have any further purpose, which is a nice way for it to end.

Sometimes we prolong relationships that have no further purpose just out of habit and psychological dependency. When there is no further karma or purpose but the relationship carries on, it's almost as if its own thrust keeps it going. So you can take a step back and discern what is really happening in the relationship to determine if it is indeed completed.

Q: **If I have had a lot of difficult things happen in my marriage, was I creating karma or balancing karma? On our honeymoon we wrecked the car and lost our luggage, and after we got home I lost my wedding ring. The same year, two close relatives died. I left him once, then returned. I left him again, and now I'm wondering if we created karma or we balanced karma!**

A: Undoubtedly, it's a karmic situation! But seriously, I think that if you left him twice, then you have to act on the basis that because you did it, it was right. That's sometimes the only proof we have that something's right: "I did it that way. That's the way I was moved to do it." And you have to have a certain trust in the inner mechanism of your being.

I can't say it was wrong for you to be married. I don't think anyone can say that. There was obviously a compelling reason. These incidences may have occurred whether you were married or not. After all, people do pass on. People do wreck cars. People do lose luggage, and all kinds of other things happen. I bet if you sat down right now, you could think of another six wonderful things that happened to you in the course of two or three years that were very lovely and beautiful.

It's unwise to be superstitious in life. If we're superstitious, where are we? We're not tying into the law of God, into the rock of our inner being.

I think that you have to be at peace with the decisions you've made. You've taken turns on the road of life. Everybody has to deal with the aftermath, the looking back, the thinking over: "Should I have done it this way? Should I have done it that way?" The more you think about it, the more you get stuck in the past. And you're not living in the past; you're living in the present. You have to go forward.

You have to believe in yourself, believe in your path, and believe that God is guiding you. Then you can say, "Okay, I've closed those doors behind me. God, open the next one. I'm ready to walk through." Be absolutely determined in your heart that the next door is going to open and you're going where you're supposed to be going. And if that person is meant to be on the other side of the door, he'll be there. And if he's not, he's not, and it's probably because you have nothing in common and won't until you are transformed and he is transformed.

So don't let doubt and fear and anxiety put a black soot on your day that causes you to second-guess yourself: "Did I or did I not do the right thing?" Have the courage to be starting anew, clean and clear.

KNOTTY RELATIONSHIPS

Q: How do I handle a relationship when the person is frequently angry and then causes me to get upset also?

A: I realized when dealing with anger many years ago that at the point of releasing anger there is a split second when you have the opportunity to decide not to vent it, not to let the anger be expressed to hurt others. And I realized that since I had that choice, if I didn't exercise that choice, I would be making tremendous karma.

And so I began the process of self-observing. When I would see myself about to express anger or irritation or any other similar thing, I realized that I must stop, change gears, and get centered. I must not allow myself to vent whatever it was.

This is one of the greatest liberations we can know—that we can be in control of our anger if we want to be, if we are determined. And it's not by forcing ourselves, but it's by internalizing the Real Self. Every day we have to decide, "Am I going to get annoyed with this person or am I going to rejoice that I can send love to that heart and consume the anger?" We must prefer a higher love to our problems, to our miseries, to our sorrows, to all of the things that beset us as human beings.

We can learn to control anger by buttoning our lips. This is a stopgap measure. You decide not to open your mouth and say something you will regret, something that will hurt someone, that will make karma, that will be an offense to the living God. It is better to fume silently than to come out with verbalizations that are costly.

You can get to the cause and core of it with inner work and therapy if needed. Why are you angry? Is it this life? Is it your parents? Is it the job you didn't get? Is it the opportunity you lost, the money you lost?

The skill of a wise therapist who understands the spiritual path is sometimes needed to help you undo old patterns and create new ones. Your soul respects a qualified professional. You can ask your Higher Self to guide you to the right therapist and to help you to work with that person. It is important to trust your intuition and your first impressions when you begin working with a therapist.

When all is said and done, you have to be determined that you are not going to be dominated or controlled by anger. The violet flame and other prayers can also help you get rid of anger. You can take a moment, pause, breathe deeply, and say from your heart, "Peace, be still, and know that I AM God!"

Q: What can I do if I am hindered by the psychology of my father
that I have taken in? My father had a very powerful personality,
and at the same time he was helpless in a lot of ways. So I feel
a block to having the trust to open my heart because I imagine
that God the Father is connected with the experience I had with
my father.

A: We can come to the point where we no longer accept the idea
that we are the way we are because of the way our parents
treated us. We may have been that way for a while, but if we're
on a spiritual path we can know that our true Father and
Mother are within. It's helpful to bring our conceptions of our
parents into perspective and to come to the place where we love
and expect nothing in return. This can bring a great sense of
freedom.

There comes a point where you have to know that ultimately love generates love. You have to prime the pump. You
start at the well, there's no water, and you keep pumping and
pumping, and finally you get water.

The flow of love is impeded if you are asking, "Did someone thank me? Did someone appreciate me? Are they going to
give back to me what I gave out?" You have to give and give
and give, and your return is not from the helpless helper, but
from the true helper—your Higher Self.

Your Higher Self understands your problem. You can communicate with that teacher. That teacher is given to you by God
and has all the answers for your life. You no longer need to feel
self-pity, bereft, alone, or indecisive.

Giving love is like being a nurse or someone who is constantly concerned with someone else's needs and always sup-
plying that need. And by and by you find that as you keep on
giving, all of a sudden all kinds of people are your friends. But
they are not possessive relationships, and God sends his love
back to you through people and through his angels. Through

all kinds of situations in life, God is always telling you how much he loves you—if you are listening.

So I think you should be at peace and accept the love of God each day. And each day you can add to your treasury more images of the father and mother, those that reflect the Father-Mother God, images that are beautiful, perhaps from the lives of the saints or others, to fill in the positive qualities lacking in your father. This will elevate his soul and bring more wholeness to you.

Q: **I am having a block to forgiving my mother because I don't respect her. My parents divorced when I was twelve and I experienced her as irresponsible and unreliable. I really want to forgive her so this doesn't affect my marriage.**

A: Can you forgive God for giving you this mother in this life?

Q: Yes.

A: Who is he?

Q: The Almighty, the presence of God, my mother's God Self? I guess I don't know.

A: You. It is the law of God working in your life, your own karma, that gave you your mother in this life. It is by your karma and your actions that you had to have this mother.

Can you forgive yourself for giving you this mother in this life? You see, really, the person you have failed to forgive is yourself. As you have sown in the past, so you have reaped, and that reaping is having her as your mother in this life.

Now, you need to first forgive yourself for your actions and the karma that gave you this mother. And when you do that, you are forgiving God, who set in motion the law of your karma. God's law of karma has worked irrevocably in your life because your very own soul demanded it.

Then you can continually pray for forgiveness for projecting upon others the traits you've found in your mother. After you do that, you can send forgiveness to your mother. You can send it on the wings of violet-flame spheres bursting with forgiveness.

Your soul has desired to see and face what it is that has held you prisoner to this planet. So God has said, "I will show you. You will come forth from the womb of your own self-created karma, your own self-created mother manifestation. You will come forth from yourself and you will face yourself. And you will see the thing you dislike most in the whole universe, which is your past misuse of the mother energies." Having it delivered unto you, you will recognize exactly that which you no longer desire to put upon God. You will love God for giving you the opportunity to see this. You will love yourself for accepting the challenge.

You will disassociate yourself from these deeds of the past and you will say, like Mark reminded us, "I made a mistake. The mistake was no good, but I am good because God made me." And then you can say to yourself, "I did all those things I see in my mother. I'm going to chase millions of violet-flame spheres after my karma. Everyone on this planet is going to be blessed because I am clearing up those things I did. And I will be so full of the forgiveness of God that I will turn, then, and face this poor woman, who herself is a prisoner of the same deeds of which I was once a prisoner. And I will flood her being with forgiveness, so much so that if it were possible, I would break the iron bands of her own karma and deliver her to her Higher Self."

This will only be possible with the consent and the striving of her free will and her soul. And if it is possible, you will pour so much forgiveness to her because you realize that she herself has imprisoned herself similarly. And perhaps even the things you did to her when she was your child in another life are the very things that are causing her to do the things she has done to you in this life.

Soon you're going to be on your knees before the Higher Self of your mother and you'll be asking your mother, "Please forgive me for my nonforgiveness. Please forgive me for whatever I have created that has created the warp in your life that made you turn around and rend me in this life."

You will have forgiven your mother by first forgiving yourself and forgiving God. Then you will have asked your mother to forgive you. This intent and act of forgiveness will start a cycle that will continue to heal your mother and the mother within you.

PART THREE

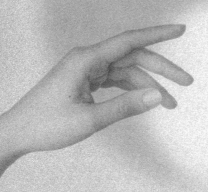

SEXUALITY
and
SPIRITUALITY

Our sexual energy can be understood
as sacred energy, or sacred fire.
It is the energy of God,
the very energy of creation.

CHAPTER 6

SEX *and* ENERGY FLOW

*A*s we see all around us, today's society is saturated with an emphasis on sex and the freedom to do whatever we want. This influences people to get caught up in expressing sexuality in various ways, which are so widespread and common that it is easy to assume that this is the only natural choice. It may seem that this is how it has always been, but this is not the case.

Numerous cultures and religions throughout history have offered timeless teachings about other choices, which include dedicating one's energies to a spiritual life. The common thread of this inner walk comes from diverse peoples from different ages and across the globe. Hindus, Buddhists, Taoists, Jews, Christians, Muslims, and others who follow a mystical path have all come to this one essential conclusion: The ultimate goal of life—and therefore the use of our life energy—is the connection and union with God.

THE SACRED FIRE

Our sexual energy can be understood as sacred energy, or sacred fire. It is the energy of God, the very energy of creation. It is the energy that blesses us with offspring as children as well as offspring of the mind and heart that come forth as creations of the Spirit. It is the creative energy that brings forth art, culture, education, science, technology, and personal fulfillment. It strengthens us, heals us physically, and enables us to bring forth our personal talents and creative genius.

This beautiful sacred fire glows as the luminosity depicted around the Buddha and the saints. The sacred fire is a garment of light that the soul requires to raise herself spiritually and connect with her Higher Self. It is the very light of our soul that becomes a magnet that little by little lessens the tenacity of our karmic ties and transforms our consciousness.

When we are born, we are given a certain portion of the sacred fire based on how we have used that energy in past lives. So we come into this life with a certain quotient of light. We can spend it and have little left, and old age can come early to people who do this. Or we can conserve this light. We can raise these sacred energies and thereby retain this light and vitality in our bodies.

The sacred fire is released not only in sexual union but it is also used every moment of our lives. It is used in everything we do and everything we create. And we are creating all the time. We expend this sacred fire through our emotions, our thoughts, our words, and our physical day-to-day activities. When it is used in sexual union, its highest culmination is in bringing forth children within the circle of a marriage dedicated to God.

The word *sex* can be understood as an abbreviation for *s*acred *e*nergy in motion, with the *x* representing the exchange or motion of the sacred fire, *s-e-x*. So the practice of sex is the use of the sacred energy of life. The purpose of sexual union is for the flow of this energy. It descends to nourish the body and then immediately rises again. This also balances the energies between man and woman in the married state.

Each descent and each rising of energy that is shared between them is ultimately for a greater realization of each one's Higher Self. The energy descends for the expression of love on this plane; it rises again for the assimilation of a higher, more beautiful awareness of the God within. So sex is much more than a simple experience between man and woman. It is an intimate experience with the light and energy of God.

My perspective on the use of the sacred fire stems from the view of the soul on the pathway to reunion with her twin flame and with her God. Therefore I don't see sex as being right or wrong or a matter of guilt and shame, but rather I see it as the energy of God. And each individual has the God-given gift of free will to determine what he will do with this energy.

SEX *and* YOUR SOUL'S INNOCENCE

The soul is clothed with veils of innocence at birth and during childhood. This innocence gives the child the ability to have an *inner sense*. This inner sense enables the child to have direct contact with his soul.

For many people nothing is more precious than a little child because the soul is so evident in the child. We love little children because they help us contact our own soul and our own beginnings, when life was sweet and we had no cares and the world was not yet upon our shoulders.

Innocence enhances the intuition of the soul and her natural desire to seek reunion with God. This sense can be retained as the child matures, gains awareness, and integrates more with her Higher Self while the sheaths of innocence are gradually removed. But when children are prematurely exposed to sexual topics, veils of innocence are removed, sometimes in abrupt or shocking ways. Over time this can desensitize the soul from her natural inclination to rise and may drive her to seek love through sexual experiences. Thus the soul's natural desire for the wholeness of the sacred fire gets translated into the desire for sex while the soul's true yearning is for the bliss of the risen sacred fire.

Parents and young people, beginning at about age twelve, need this understanding of the sacred fire. They need to understand that sex as it is practiced on earth today is imposed upon people as the ultimate human experience, and this message permeates our culture through the media, music, and education. People become indoctrinated to believe that they are not normal unless they have frequent sex or engage in other sexual habits. These ever-present messages are automatically absorbed by people, particularly the youth, who are especially vulnerable.

THE SEVEN CHAKRAS *and the* SACRED FIRE

How do we restore the soul's innocence and wholeness? How do we preserve and expand the sacred fire rather than spend it in ways that our modern culture portrays?

The sacred fire within us moves according to a science of energy flow. Whether we are married, celibate, or somewhere in between, the life-giving flow of this energy is a key to our vitality and wholeness.

When we are born, the sacred fire is naturally rising on the altar of the spine. It has a beautiful ascending and descending pattern and our whole body is nourished by this light. The organs are nourished. We have unlimited energy. We learn to crawl. We learn to walk. We are absorbing a vast amount of knowledge. And we are developing in leaps and bounds because this sacred energy is in us. We are endowed with it. And depending on our past lives, we may have a tremendous amount of light or we may have a lesser light.

This light flows through the *chakras,* or spiritual energy centers, within the body. The chakras (Sanskrit: 'wheel' or 'disc') are energy centers that correspond to different glands and areas of the body. These dynamic energy centers constantly take in, store, and send out spiritual energy and light. This light-energy has been called the vital force, life energy, or prana. In other words, chakras are sending and receiving stations of energy.[1] (See Plate 6.)

At every moment, a crystal clear stream of life descends to us from our God Presence to our Higher Self. This energy is distributed first to our heart chakra and then to our other chakras. The chakras act as transformers for this life energy, this spiritual light, invigorating our memory, our mind, our feelings, and desires, as well as the very cells and organs of our physical body.

There are seven major chakras: the crown, third eye, throat, heart, solar plexus, seat of the soul, and base of the spine. Situated along the spinal column, they are invisible to the physical eye, yet our life and spiritual progress depend on their vitality.

Each chakra has a unique function and frequency and represents a different quality of God's consciousness, which we are intended to emulate and absorb as we evolve on our spiritual journey. These differences are denoted by the color and the number of petals of each chakra. The more petals a chakra has, the higher its frequency. And the more energy that flows through a chakra, the faster it spins.

By our negative interactions with others throughout our many lifetimes, karmic debris has accumulated around our chakras. This debris is like the leaves that plug a drain after it rains. In order for water to run through the drain properly, we need to clear away the leaves.

Similarly, in order for God's light to flow through our chakras, we need to clear the debris that clings to those sacred centers. When our chakras are clogged, we may feel sluggish, pessimistic, or sick without knowing why. When our chakras and the circuits of energy that connect them are clear, we feel more energetic, positive, joyful, and giving.

As we develop spiritually, the chakras go through an evolution-ary process. They range from small and dormant to fully awakened, when they emit much light. These centers can look different in dif-ferent people, depending on their past and present use of energy and their stage of spiritual development.

Just as we breathe in and out through our mouth, so all of the chakras are taking in and giving forth the energies of God according to the frequency of each specific chakra. As light streams forth from our chakras, it forms a radiating energy field, or aura, that penetrates and extends beyond the boundaries of our physical form. Through these seven centers of being, we can send light to the planet.

We experience the energy in each of the chakras in a unique way. For example, the love in our heart chakra inspires us with the compassion and generosity to lovingly care for others. When we are focused on studying, our energy is centered in the crown chakra, where we contact the mind of God and receive sudden flashes of illumination or clear insights.

The uniqueness of each chakra manifests in specific character-istics. The **crown chakra** is the chakra of illumination, which regu-lates the mental faculties and memory. It is yellow and is located at the top, or crown, of the head. It has 972 petals, which is reflected in its name the "thousand-petaled lotus." The enlightenment of the Buddha comes with the release of the light of the crown chakra. It is the experience of knowing all things without being tutored or taught.

The **third-eye chakra** is below the crown chakra at the center of the brow. It is emerald green when purified and has ninety-six petals. The third-eye chakra is intended to anchor the vision of God, the vision of perfection. A purified third-eye chakra enables us to see with our inner eye, to have the gift of inner sight.

Next is the **throat chakra**, which is located over the physical throat. It has sixteen petals and is blue in color. It is the power chakra, or the place of empowerment, through which large quantities of energy are expressed through man's unique ability of speech. With the disciplined use of the power of the throat chakra in prayer, mantras, and other forms of the spoken word, we can make significant progress on the spiritual path.

The central and most important organ of your body is your heart and, likewise, the central and most important chakra is the twelve-petaled **heart chakra**. The very energy of life is distributed from the heart chakra to the other chakras as well as to all the cells and nerve centers of your body. It is where the pink fires of love burn brightly from within us. The heart chakra is extremely sensitive and should be guarded from negative energies, such as anger or irritation.

The **solar plexus** is the first chakra below the heart. It has ten petals and its colors are a combination of rich purple and metallic gold. It is located at the navel and corresponds to a nearby nerve center. Most of us have felt "butterflies" or that familiar discomfort "in the pit of the stomach." The solar plexus and the throat

Crown Chakra

Third-Eye Chakra

Throat Chakra

Heart Chakra

Solar-Plexus Chakra

Seat-of-the-Soul Chakra

Base-of-the-Spine Chakra

chakras are closely linked. As soon as the solar plexus is agitated, the pitch and the volume of the voice often goes up. Feelings of agitation or fear as well as feelings of peace and devotion are filtered through this center.

It is at the solar plexus where our soul learns to cultivate inner peace by mastering her emotions and desires while contending with the tests of her karma. Mastering emotions does not mean that we have no emotion. Emotion *(e-motion)* is simply *energy in motion*. We can use our energy in motion to amplify positive or discordant feelings. It is the love and fire of the heart that is required to master our emotions and the energy of the solar plexus.

The **seat-of-the-soul chakra** is located halfway between the navel and the base of the spine, and it is the abiding place of the soul. This chakra governs the flow of light and karmic patterns in the genes and chromosomes and in the sperm and the egg of man and woman. It is a six-petaled, violet chakra, and it's called the chakra of freedom because violet is the color of freedom, transmutation, and forgiveness. When we are able to connect with our soul through this chakra, we gain a greater sense of intuition, which is like having a sixth sense. For instance, it can be a self-protective sense that lets us know when something is not right. Such intuitive soul senses can be developed with practice.

The last of the seven chakras is the **base-of-the-spine chakra**, which contains the sacred fire of the Mother light, called the kundalini in Eastern tradition. The vitality of the base-of-the-spine chakra affects all the other chakras. Some qualities of this chakra are purity, harmony, order, and symmetry. Its color is white and it has four petals.

THE KUNDALINI ENERGIES

Three energies of the kundalini rise from the base-of-the-spine chakra and flow in and around the spine. In Sanskrit these are called the *idā, pingalā,* and *sushumnā.* The sushumna flows through the center of the spinal column; the ida and pingala are on the outside, carrying feminine and masculine currents. With each lifetime, male or female, we are given a certain charge of the kundalini energies at the base-of-the-spine chakra. The ida and pingala currents around the spinal column carry a different charge depending on whether you are male or female.

The kundalini energies rise naturally from the base-of-the-spine chakra as your chakras are purified and the love in your heart expands. As the kundalini rises, each chakra experiences the effect of this light and the chakras in turn begin to spin. They raise their petals, signifying the unfoldment of our latent spiritual powers whereby we can begin to have deep inner experiences in the mysteries of God. For the chakras are sacred centers for God-awareness.

The soul's natural state is wholeness, and this is maintained by raising the Mother light from the base of the spine to the crown, where it merges with the light of the Father. Balancing factors, such as exercise, hatha yoga, meditation, the right food, fresh air, and communion with nature contribute to the flow of light through the chakras. The light can also be raised through specific meditations as well as prayer and, most importantly, the purification of the heart and other chakras with the violet flame. Everything we do to allow this flow will benefit us, including giving us greater intuition and soul awareness.

When the sacred fire in the base-of-the-spine chakra is conserved and consecrated to life, it is pulsating and rising. Depending on how a person has garnered this light, the flow is large or small. If the currents of the kundalini are weakened by inordinate or excessive sexual practices, then the balancing and raising of our energies is diminished and the soul's path to wholeness and reunion with her Real Self is impeded.

For example, the practice in tantric yoga in which a male and female face one another and meditate on each other's eyes to force the raising of this light would not be recommended. Forcing the kundalini to rise prematurely before our chakras are balanced and cleared can activate negative energies, especially in the lower chakras. Therefore it can interfere with our spiritual progress.

The kundalini will rise gradually on its own when the flow is unobstructed and when we use spiritual exercises to raise the Mother light. The sacred energies will flow safely upward because that is the natural course of energy. It is God's energy and it is returning to him. (See Chapter 8.)

THE REJUVENATION *of the* SACRED FIRE

The chakras above the heart have the masculine (plus) polarity, corresponding to the energies of the Father. The chakras below the heart have the feminine (minus) polarity, corresponding to the energies of the Mother.

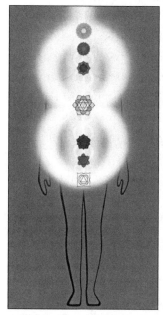

Figure-Eight Flow of Energy through the Chakras

You can visualize the flow of these energies as a figure eight, with the top circle representing the upper chakras and the bottom circle representing the lower chakras. The nexus where they meet represents the heart chakra.

In this figure-eight flow, the energies move clockwise from the top of the upper circle through the connecting point of the heart and then down to the bottom of the lower circle. Then they move counterclockwise back up again. The light of the lower chakras rises to energize the upper chakras, and the spiritual light of God descends to cleanse the lower chakras. In this flow, the upper chakras are nourished for the expansion of God's consciousness in us, the light is continually raised, and we are continually rejuvenated. At the nexus, our hearts can become a fountain of love, even an overwhelming love for others. We can feel this intense love and expand this love by sending it to bless all life.

A certain fulfillment of wholeness occurs in each chakra when the light from the Father, our own God Presence, descends and infuses our chakras with the masculine polarity and the Mother light rises with the feminine polarity. This union of masculine and feminine energies is intended to take place not alone in the base-of-the-spine chakra but in all of the seven chakras. It is a union of God with God in every chakra that produces wholeness, and it can be sustained hour by hour.

In this way we can joyously pursue the desire for wholeness, and we can experience it without the unnecessary expenditure of the sacred fire. Excessive sexual activity drains us of our energy, and this may not even be according to our conscious will or determination. But it may be provoked by the outer stimulus of the world, through the media and a culture focused on sex and pleasure. With the expansion of love and the use of the violet flame and other meditations, we can reestablish the natural flow of energy in our chakras.

Since we live in a civilization that promotes promiscuity, we may not have received teaching about striving for the mastery of energy. So when we have sexual desires, it may not be that these are impure or wrong desires. Rather, our desires have not been cultivated according to a divine design and a divine standard. Yet just about every desire that we have can be cultivated into a God-desire. For the same energies that contribute to the desire for a sexual encounter can instead, when spiritualized, purify us, heal us physically and in all ways, and empower us with the full use of these energies in our chakras.

The raising of these same energies will also contribute to fulfilling your God-desire to reunite with your twin flame. When you keep your chakras trimmed with light, garnering the energy that would otherwise be spent in sex, your chakras are like beacon lights shining in the windows of your being.

Somewhere across the margent of the world, someone, perhaps your twin flame, may also be garnering energy and light in the chakras. When you reach the peak of that perfect pitch where your chakras sing with the energy of God focused there, you will find your divine counterpart if that one is also focusing that energy at a certain peak and pitch. And you will come together by a union of spiritual energies, which is not to say that you will not also experi-ence physical, emotional, and mental attraction. For union takes place on all planes.

CHAPTER 7

SEXUAL RELATIONSHIPS *and* PRACTICES

*O*nce I was talking with some teenage girls about the fact that it's nice to be going out with good-looking young men and to have a good time. But the question is, when they say, "I love you," do they have the capacity to really know you? Are they saying that they truly love your soul?

That is the most precious part of the love of twin flames. It's not merely an outer attraction, although there can certainly be a great pull and attraction between twin flames. But what is most profound about twin flames is the deep love for the real essence of each other's soul.

The experience of having become farther and farther from our twin flame and that deep love is painful for our soul. So part of seeking our twin flame is to resolve the pain and the experience of separation. But we usually don't consciously remember what we have lost or what we are looking for. Thus our search for a perfect love can lead to shallow sexual encounters, spending our life force, our light, and separating more from our twin flame.

Your light is one of the ways that your twin flame can recognize you. And by the light of your twin flame and your own light, you also recognize that beloved one. It would be tragic if you were in the same room with your twin flame and you had no recognition of him because you had spent your light and, as a result, your inner soul and spiritual faculties were not quickened to the level of sensitivity needed for that recognition.

SEXUAL ATTRACTIONS

You may remember an outstanding love, perhaps a first love in your late teens or twenties, when you felt you had a special connection with someone. It may have been a pure love, with genuine care and appreciation for one another. Or perhaps you discovered that it was only a sensual attraction and you became disillusioned. When you're navigating through relationships, you may go through a difficult learning process, but by careful observation of yourself and others, you can refine your discernment about the true nature of an attraction.

In the course of this lifetime, you will meet dozens of people you have been married to in past lives and with whom you've had sexual relations. These encounters naturally take place because there is an energy to be balanced between the two of you. Although you will inevitably meet such people, this is not necessarily a sign of an enduring alliance with a constructive purpose.

An instant attraction doesn't automatically mean that now you've met your twin flame or your soul mate. Rather, it may be a sign that on your way back to God you have karma to be balanced. Sometimes the attraction is more powerful and exhilarating than sex itself. People can believe that by the intensity of the attraction it must be real, instead of seeing that by the intensity of the attraction it must be unreal. So we may have sexual attractions to people even when we realize that they're not good for us. Perhaps we feel an inequality with them, that they're somehow far more evolved than we are or that we are way beyond them. We may consistently have negative feelings in their presence. When we sense such things, it helps to remember that we have made karma with people, very binding karma. Strong attractions may indicate a tremendous need for love to resolve this kind of intense karma.

An attraction can be so overwhelming that we feel we cannot fight against it, so it becomes a sexual relationship. Such an attraction may begin in appreciation and care, but it may end in anger or aggression because we haven't grown enough to balance the karma and heal the relationship. Thus a sexual interchange does not necessarily balance karma at all. It is the sacred fire of the heart's love that balances karma, and you can give that love by your sincere effort for the elevation of the other person.

There are many different types of sexual attractions because the energy involved could be an expenditure of energy in one or more of the chakras. Following is a story of a woman who got caught up in the misuse of energy through the allure of eye contact.

Karla was in her early twenties, unmarried, lonely, and hoping for the right man to come along. She felt that no one in her life deeply knew or understood her. Well, just as the universe would have it—to teach and to test her— a handsome young man with piercing blue eyes joined the company where she was working and the two became friends. Karla felt that when this man looked at her with those beautiful eyes, he could read her soul, a feeling she longed for, and so she developed a strong attraction to him. She thought the attraction was mutual because there had developed between them a strong habit of eye contact, providing some sense of gratifying titillation between them. After some time, Karla finally realized that what was really happening was an exchange of sexual energies

through the eyes—a means of an energy exchange with no
personal satisfaction, nothing that acknowledged her soul,
as Karla had thought. It was simply another way for two
people lacking interior wholeness to share in a shallow
and impersonal connection, in this case leaving Karla with
only more feelings of emptiness. Nothing ever came of the
relationship, but she learned a good lesson.

Attractions can be amplified by other factors, such as behaviors and habits of dress, flirting, and the many male-female interactions that are displayed as normal in our culture. Men and women can rationalize their ingrained habits in a thousand different ways that keep them bound to a lower consciousness.

We can also be drawn to people who have a magnetic, charismatic personality based on glamour and sensual appeal. Some people in the field of entertainment have these traits. They may have eyes with a magnetic quality; however, it is not the magnetism of God but rather the magnetism of the lower nature. Various types of people have personal magnetism because they are spending their light and energy in misusing the sacred fire and this shows in their aura. It can seem like light, but it is the magnetism of spent light that draws people to them.

On the other hand, people who radiate vibrant, joyful, spiritual energy can have an attractive quality of pure light. We can be attracted to the opposite sex in a healthy, nonerotic way. It is an energetic attraction of the joy of being in polarity with our highest love on the other side of the universe, so to speak.

HOW *to* MASTER SEXUAL ATTRACTIONS

When we find ourself having a strong attraction to someone, we can take a few steps back and give ourself a break from the intensity of the relationship. We can go into nature or to another place of comfort. We can talk with a trusted friend or relative. We can enter our hearts and deeply listen to what our intuition is telling us about this relationship.

We can also pray and call to Archangel Michael, since he is the archangel who protects us and delivers us from harm. He has delivered me from the most difficult circumstances, and he comes with his sword of powerful blue flame to cut us free from all types of dangers and trying situations, including unhealthy relationships. If you want to be free and you want to let go of a relationship, pray to him with the simple call, "Archangel Michael, help me!" so that he can cut you free from the pull that you can't seem to get past. Then you can literally walk away from it, and you can appeal to God to help you resolve any residual issues connected with that relationship.

You can get through balancing this karma without engaging in former misuses of the sacred fire. For example, when you meet this person, you might notice the energy between the two of you and you might say to yourself, "Now, this is a sensual attraction. It may not be enduring. I'm going to pray for the transmutation of any past karma and really work at this. And once I have done this for a certain period of time, then I'll see if there's anything left of the relationship." Many times you will find that the relationship has dissolved before you have even gotten involved and you have saved yourself from heartbreak and making more karma.

On the journey homeward, we will encounter every seed that we have sown in the past. We need these encounters because they provide the opportunity for us and the other person to balance that karma so that a resolution can be reached. And therefore we can move forward on our path with a greater lightness in our step, for a pack of karma upon our back has been lifted.

If all of us, especially the youth, only knew these principles of twin flames, soul mates, and karmic relationships, how much we could be spared!

PREMARITAL SEX

From the perspective of the soul, premarital sexual relations can be a detour to finding your higher love. Living with someone or having an affair can add a weight of karma that can impede finding love with the right partner. You may share your karma for a while and pool your resources for a worthwhile or enjoyable experience, but when you go your separate ways, you go back to your separate karma without having balanced more of it.

While a couple is living together, they share their karma without the circle of protection that marriage provides and they are not able to mutually balance their karma as they would in the oneness of the marriage relationship. If the couple parts, they carry the extra karma of their previous boyfriend or girlfriend. Thus it becomes an added weight. They may also suffer the painful experience of a relationship that has not included the sincere love, acceptance, and fulfillment of a healthy committed marriage, as this young woman expresses.

As a twenty-six year old woman living in today's world, I have made a few mistakes when it comes to relationships. Before I was mature enough to make good decisions, I became sexually active because it's almost impossible to date someone and avoid it. This has been a painful experience that has left me with many feelings of rejection rather than feelings of being loved. And it has left its scars. It has taken me years to even acknowledge that I had this pain. Sex is such a casual thing these days that I considered it normal and had no idea what the emotional cost would be.

I have given up on shallow and meaningless relationships that leave me feeling empty, and while this has been a wonderful healing process, it has also been very isolating at the same time. It takes a lot of time to heal.

When people have premarital relationships, most of their sexual involvements are simply an exchange of energies at the karmic level. They take on the subconscious karmic patterns of the misqualified energy of their partner and these remain with them. However, within the consecrated circle of marriage and its sealing in God, a couple helps each other to bear their karma through their transforming love. The married couple has the opportunity, through spiritual attunement and raising up their energies in meditation, to spiritualize their union.

If sexual intercourse is not spiritualized, the two individuals may indeed experience physical pleasure. But taking on each other's karmic patterns can have negative effects that can burden the soul.

When we invest our energies in premarital sex, we allow another person to be in a position of polarity with us for the exchange of the sacred fire. This involves a law of energy related to polarity—the feminine energies pass to the male, and masculine energies pass to the female. And when sex is not spiritualized, the polarity often wears out and we seek another partner who has a greater magnetism or energy flow. This magnetism is sensual rather than spiritual.

PROMISCUITY *and* SEXUAL OVERINDULGENCE

Just as premarital sex increases a person's karmic burden because of taking on the subconscious karmic patterns of the partner, this karmic weight would be multiplied in promiscuity and sexual overindulgence. In these practices the energy and light of the sacred fire is continually dissipated.

The soul requires this energy, this sacred fire, in order to rise to a higher level of consciousness. The spending of this energy can block the natural attunement of the soul with her Higher Self. Thus the soul can be deprived of the inner bliss of the heaven-world. This is the great loss, not because of sin or the sense of sin, but because these sexual experiences can become a wedge between the soul and God.

Promiscuity may be related to the identity crisis suffered by those who have intimate relationships on a casual basis. They can take on the karmic identities of so many other people that they no longer know who they really are. The excessive spending of energies also drains the chakras of light and can result in psychological issues.[1]

Because of loneliness and because they do not have the spiritual perspective presented to them, people satiate themselves in the activities of this life, which may include promiscuity. They keep themselves going twenty-four hours a day because when everything stops they are still left with a gnawing, a loneliness. This is felt by the soul who has not been satisfied through an experience of spiritual bliss, which can be a daily occurrence when the light is raised.

The other problem with promiscuity is that the desire for sex can become addictive. The more people spend of their vital energies, the more they may seek sexual encounters to fill the emptiness, and this can become a vicious circle. It is the need for the sacred fire, which has been spent. This can lead to social problems, such as seeking sexual stimulation from pornography or even engaging in sexually violent acts of rape or abuse.

It's sad to see people caught up in this situation, because it's difficult for them to break the chain of this habit of casual sex, which is sex for the sake of sex with no emotional fulfillment. Some people get so caught up in this that they can look decades older than others their age because of the tremendous loss of their life force as well as the emotional harm they have experienced.

ENERGIES CARVE DEEP CHANNELS

In our modern civilization, most people have a buildup of energy in the lower chakras, the chakras below the heart. Although people are not consciously aware of it, they are often experiencing energies that are blocked, excessive, or distributed unevenly through their chakras. People feel this pressure of energy and they want a release, so they look for various ways of dealing with it.

We can dissipate this energy in any one of our chakras through various activities. While some people handle this imbalance of energy through sex, others refrain from sex but engage in other ways of releasing the energy, such as criticizing, lying, and sending forth anger. Drinking, smoking, and excessive eating, including consuming too much sugar, all may relate to the individual's attempt to deal with energies that are not in a state of flow. These habits are a release of energy through the lower chakras or a misqualification of the upper chakras. And such habits, including sexual ones, can be carried over from lifetime to lifetime.

So from past use, man has carved within himself deep channels into which he has directed the energies of the sacred fire in both positive and negative ways. Some may have a habit of directing this energy to the crown chakra, and they are often devoted to learning and teaching. Others have directed it to the heart center, sending it as love to their fellow man. Other people have directed the flow of the sacred fire largely through the base-of-the-spine and seat-of-the-soul chakras; therefore, out of habit, the sacred energies of God that flow to them are being directed subconsciously to the lower chakras. Although this may be experienced as a problem with sex, it is really a problem of energy flow.

When we habitually express irritation, anger, or a misuse of sexual energy, we are carving a deep pattern of negative energy within ourselves. But we can decide to redirect that energy, to close off one channel and open up another. For example, when we have the habit of gossiping, we can gently but firmly cease our conversation. We can then engage in another activity that is more productive. We might even use the throat chakra in another way—in singing, in giving prayers, decrees, or mantras. When we do this, we may be aware of a rising and expansion of our energy, which may be noticeably different from the subtle depletion of energy that we felt before. In this way, we are forming new habit patterns.

SEXUAL HABITS THAT SPEND *the* LIGHT

Again, I don't think of sex as right or wrong, but I think of it as the energy of God. God gives us the gift of free will, so we have the freedom to choose how we use the sacred fire and our sexual energies. And for some this can understandably be challenging. We may have unwanted sexual habits from past lifetimes, and it takes patience to begin to change them. In addition, we have been programmed by today's culture to believe that in order to be balanced it is fine to be sexually indulgent.

Some sexual habits that are accepted and touted as natural, even healthy, are not seen that way from a spiritual perspective. Masturbation is one example. This habit is often accompanied by sexual fantasies, which focuses one's attention only on sexual desires. The energy is spent—the same energy, the kundalini, that could be raised for God-inspired and creative expression. When this energy is conserved, it increases one's strength and vitality.

Oral sex is another practice that misdirects energy, whether the couple is married or not. Most people do not realize that this is so, and therefore they think that there is no problem with it. It is especially important for people seeking a higher love to understand that this practice causes the flow of energy to move downward rather than to spiral upward to Spirit. This is due to the polarity of energies in the chakras.

When the chakras of a man and woman are aligned—the upper chakras with the upper chakras and the lower chakras with the lower chakras—the masculine and feminine polarity in each chakra is exchanged and the sacred fire can rise. During oral sex, the upper chakras are positioned with the lower chakras at a time when the sacred energies are being released for creation. The kundalini is not raised and the energies stay centered in the lower chakras. The more one's energy is spent in this downward release, the more this practice depletes the light.

While viewing pornography is not physically engaging in sex, lustfully looking at pornography also spends the sacred fire. Where the attention goes, there one's energy goes. So the energies of the chakras become engaged, even if that person is not physically involved in sex. By having sexual feelings, a person is still dissipating a certain amount of energy.

TRANSFORMING HABITS

When we first realize that we have been misusing our energy in ways and degrees that are detrimental, it may be easy to be critical of ourselves. But the misuse is understandable if we develop such habits when we're not aware that they are problematic, when we don't know why or how to change them, and when they are reinforced, indeed encouraged, in the culture all around us.

When we have a greater understanding, we can rejoice in our new knowledge and be patient with ourselves as we go through the process of changing those habits. With the realization that sexual habits are a matter of energy flow, we can experiment with changing that energy flow. We have the opportunity to redirect, raise, and expand the energy, the light, within us. Gaining self-mastery in this way can be an exciting and rewarding experience. Just think what a difference it can make for you when you take charge of the marvelous light of God that flows through you every day!

Although it is important to be aware of our biological needs and desires, we do not have to be governed by our inordinate desires or habits of seeking pleasure. We have the free will to choose how we relate to life and to redirect what we consider to be our lesser desires into higher expressions of God-desire for the fulfillment of our spiritual aspirations.

We all know that it is a lot easier to run downhill than it is to walk uphill, and it is much easier to swim with the human current than to move in the opposite direction. This can also be the way it is when we decide we want to break a negative habit.

How do we start forming a good habit? We start forming it by doing it. Whatever we do that is truly beneficial, that brings about beneficial results, we can do again. The more we repeat the good habit, the more the groove deepens within our memory. And as the groove gets deeper, we will tend to repeat this habit more easily.

The first thing we can do is affirm for ourselves that we want to break a certain habit. We might ask ourselves how we started the habit in the first place, and the answer, of course, is that we started this habit by doing it. In order to break the habit, we simply have to start by telling ourselves that we do not want to do it anymore. This establishes our motivation and will.

So we stop doing it once, and then we stop doing it twice. And after a while we realize that we do not need this habit anymore, and this becomes instilled in our memory. This provides momentum for the next day and the next day. Every day that we create a good momentum, we're creating a good momentum for the next day. It's one day at a time. And if we need to change our friends in order to reinforce the change we desire for ourselves, then that is what we do.

The root of man's desire is based upon the depth of the groove that he has cut within his memory. Therefore in order to eradicate unwanted habits, we should allow time for this change to occur. Changing these habits may be gradual or immediate, so we need to be patient with ourselves. We need to understand that such habits are developed because of misuses of the natural ways of life, and so we desire to be restored to the path that nature intends. In this process we can allow ourselves to be free from unnecessary feelings of guilt.

The violet flame is the most direct and efficient means of transforming habits and clearing the channels so that the light may rise as a stream though the chakras. Without this clearing, at each stop along the way, like a subway station, there are accumulations, and therefore the Mother light cannot rise unobstructed. The soul is meant to rise, to follow the stream, yet the stream cannot rise because of the karmic conditions that result from the misuse of the light in the seven chakras. We can simply trust in God and invoke this blessed violet flame to purify our memories, thoughts, feelings, and desires, that our light and life may be restored. Our love and determination to be the fullness of our own true nature and to help others is the goad and the strength for new levels of self-mastery.

CHAPTER 8

PRACTICAL KEYS *for* RAISING *the* SACRED FIRE

*P*erhaps you haven't found the one you want to share your life with. You may find this person soon or maybe not for years. In the meantime, how can you prepare yourself? The answer is simple—raise the sacred fire.

During the course of our everyday life, we can raise the sacred fire in simple but effective ways. We can raise it to our heart chakra and send it forth to others as expressions of love and gratitude. We can raise the sacred fire to our throat chakra to comfort a friend with kind words and to offer prayers for those in need. With the sacred fire raised to our third-eye chakra, we can perceive the divine nature in a coworker or child and envision the creation of beautiful works of art.

There are practical ways to raise this energy, starting with physical exercise. Since energy gets clogged by lack of exercise, it is helpful to engage regularly in your favorite sport. A hearty workout, doing laps at the local pool, a good hard game of basketball or volleyball, skiing, hatha yoga—real physical exercise that gets the oxygen flowing through your heart and bloodstream—will loosen the energy in your body and keep it flowing between your chakras.

MEDITATION *on the* RESURRECTION FLAME

Another key to raising the sacred fire is using the spiritual light of the beautiful resurrection flame. We have all had moments when we felt uplifted with a sense of vibrant life. It may have been seeing a newborn baby for the first time, feeling the fresh grass under our bare feet, or hearing a chorus of birds on a spring morning. This sense of renewal, hope, and buoyancy is an effect of the resurrection flame.

Within our heart there is a spark of life that comes from the Creator's own heart. It is a spiritual fire that burns as a triune essence of divine love, wisdom, and power. When this threefold flame expands and begins to whirl, its plumes of pink, yellow, and blue blend as one flame, having the rainbow iridescence of the mother-of-pearl. Thus the accelerated threefold flame becomes the resurrection flame. Arising from God's flame of life within our heart, it is a bubbling fountain, a life-giving force of rebirth and rejuvenation.

Saints and sages of East and West have had such mastery of the energy of this resurrection flame that they have been able to restore life to those who required healing. Such healings have been called miracles, while it was the God-given power of the magnified and accelerated threefold flame within their heart that was the source of these life-giving transformations.

To start the action of the resurrection flame, you can visualize yourself standing in a pillar of swirling spirals of opalescent rainbow light while giving the following mantra. Remember that when we say "I AM," we are affirming, "God in me is."

**I AM the resurrection and the life of every cell and atom
of my being now made manifest!**

"I AM the resurrection and the life" is the mantra that will raise the sacred fire. It can be followed by any wording that indicates where you want that resurrection flame directed, perhaps for healing.

To heal your heart, for example, you can meditate on your heart and give the mantra "I AM the resurrection and the life of every cell and atom of my heart now made manifest!" This invokes the rainbow rays of the resurrection flame within and around the heart. The activity of this spiritual fire restores the balance of forces necessary for the proper flow of light and healing within each cell, molecule, and atom of the physical heart. This can be done for other people as well, inserting their name and the condition that requires healing. Wherever this light is invoked, there *is* resurrection.

Imagine that your spine is a thermometer and the base-of-the-spine chakra is like the round part at the base of the thermometer. This is where the energies of the Mother light, the kundalini, are locked. You can visualize the energy of that chakra taking on the quality of the resurrection flame, rising up your spine, and raising all the energy that causes a burden in the lower chakras. Rather than the suppression of energy, this is the true translation, or transmutation, of energy into divine creativity.

MEDITATION *on the* SECRET LOVE STAR

Along with the resurrection flame, the meditation on the secret love star can help raise the sacred fire from the lower chakras to the upper chakras. The secret love star is the star of your God Presence, and it is a pulsating cosmic light. In this meditation it is the lodestone, the focus, for pulling up the energies of your lower chakras. So this pull that you're going to feel, this magnetization of energy, comes from the secret love star.

This meditation is done in a standing position. Raise both of your arms, and then envision and feel yourself taking the energy from your heart and placing it above your head as a star. The heart is the source of all that you create. You can take the energy from your heart and create anything your heart desires.

Reach high for the star first with your right hand. At the same time, feel a pulling from your right foot all the way up your side. All of your muscles are pulling to raise the energy to reach the star. The energy of your being is spiraling up as the resurrection flame along your spine to the star above.

Then give the mantra "I AM the resurrection and the life of every cell and atom of my being now made manifest!"

Next, bring your right arm down, and push up with the left side, doing the same thing that you did with the right side.

Continue alternating the two sides. Give the mantra for each side as you reach and stretch on that side for the star. As you are reaching and stretching, feel yourself releasing and raising the sacred fire from your lower chakras.

You can give this mantra or do this meditation three times, nine times, or twelve times a day, whatever you feel you need. It only takes a minute or two to stand up and give this meditation.

Sometimes when you first begin to direct the light through your body in this way, you might feel a stirring up of sexual energies and desires. This is simply because the light is activating movement and flow, and some of this flow wants to go into the old channels. If this happens, you can continue the resurrection mantra and feel the spiritual light in the upper chakras exerting a pulling action on your lower chakras, and eventually you can feel a transformation of that energy.

VIOLET-FLAME MEDITATION
to PURIFY *the* CHAKRAS

Another way to raise the sacred fire is to place your attention on purifying the chakras as you give decrees and affirmations to the violet flame. The following is a specific violet-flame meditation to purify your chakras.

We begin our meditation with the heart chakra since spiritual light from our Higher Self descends first into this chakra. Next it is distributed to the other six chakras and then to the rest of the body. As you give this meditation, see a violet-colored flame bathing and cleansing each chakra.

You can begin the meditation with the following prayer.

In the name of my own God Presence, I call for the purification of my chakras. According to God's will, I decree:

I AM a being of violet fire!
I AM the purity God desires!*

My heart is a chakra of violet fire,
My heart is the purity God desires!

I AM a being of violet fire!
I AM the purity God desires!

My throat chakra is a wheel of violet fire,
My throat chakra is the purity God desires!

I AM a being of violet fire!
I AM the purity God desires!

My solar plexus is a sun of violet fire,
My solar plexus is the purity God desires!

I AM a being of violet fire!
I AM the purity God desires!

My third eye is a center of violet fire,
My third eye is the purity God desires!

I AM a being of violet fire!
I AM the purity God desires!

My soul chakra is a sphere of violet fire,
My soul is the purity God desires!

---

*For greater effectiveness you can give each two-line mantra three times or more.

I AM a being of violet fire!
I AM the purity God desires!

My crown chakra is a lotus of violet fire,
My crown chakra is the purity God desires!

I AM a being of violet fire!
I AM the purity God desires!

My base chakra is a fount of violet fire,
My base chakra is the purity God desires!

I AM a being of violet fire!
I AM the purity God desires!

CELIBACY *and* RAISING *the* SACRED FIRE

Whether you are single or married, the path of celibacy is one way to raise and preserve the sacred fire. Being celibate can mean that you are raising the energies in your being and dedicating them to God.

It has been the belief of spiritual teachers for thousands of years that the celibate rises higher in consciousness and has more God consciousness than someone who is married. However, the married person who spiritualizes sex in marriage can also attain great enlightenment and heights of awareness. By practicing ways to raise the sacred energies, the married person who has a spiritual consciousness can rise just as high as the celibate if he will put his mind to it and if he will determine that God is first in his life. (See Chapter 10.)

As mentioned earlier, strenuous exercise can be helpful when you pursue periods of celibacy. Then you can go to bed at the end of the day feeling physically spent. You can also give the meditation to the secret love star or invoke the violet flame. Many people use these simple methods to live a balanced celibate life.

The blessing of the celibate path while you are single is that it can bring you closer to your highest love if that is what you desire. You will have raised the light in your chakras so that you will be the magnet for that love. I have watched as people have raised and transformed their energies in the way that I have described for perhaps a few months, six months, or a year. By doing so they have often attracted a person who reflects and complements the best part of themselves.

In marriages, with mutual consent, a husband and wife can have natural intervals of sexual relations as well as periods of celibacy. In addition to the abiding love shared between a husband and wife, marriage is also a contract, and each party in the contract has certain needs and rights. The give-and-take of the sexual relationship is part of that contract.

Therefore in the midst of a marriage, if someone decides that he is going to become celibate, he needs to do so in consultation with his spouse. If he wishes to pursue celibacy and the spouse does not, then the marriage may not be congruent with its original contract. This is something that many people do not realize. They feel that if they decide to be celibate, they can simply announce to their spouse, "I'm going to be celibate and you can fend for yourself."

Instead, the couple can sit down and say, "Now, this is what I expect of marriage. This is the kind of person I am. These are my habits."

It's natural to have sexual desires, which are inherent to the bodies we live in and are also affected by habits from past lives. On our spiritual journey these desires can change over time. For example, they can be sublimated or transformed by service or other creative endeavors. Our love may be such that we want to take some of the energy of our desires and channel it for the good of those around us.

An uplifting and harmonious marriage can be one in which you evolve together in your love and in the disciplining of your energies. You can think of the uses of the sacred fire as being like a ladder.

You can find your rung on the ladder and continue to aspire to the next rung, not because of guilt or shame but because it's the law of your evolving souls. This may involve mutual periods of celibacy. So while we meet our needs for a sexual relationship as well as for comfort, security, establishing a household, and raising children, something else can be occurring in the marriage. We are balancing karma and evolving in marriage to bless life in a larger sense.

THE PRACTICE *of* SURRENDER

As we strive to raise the sacred fire and transform certain aspects of our lives, another helpful tool is the practice of surrender.

In this surrender we turn over to God every aspect of our life, including all unwanted habits, and we ask for our desires to become God-desire. We withhold nothing from him. If we are not sure if someone is right for us, for example, we can put the situation in God's hands and trust that he will take care of it. This can save us a lot of trouble, because we don't want for ourselves what God does not want for us. If we surrender our will to him, we will be blessed with all that is best for us and all that is meant to be ours.

You can sit down and write a letter to God, saying, "I surrender..." and then you can list all the different things you would like to surrender to God. Doing this can bring you a great sense of peace. A special prayer you can give is the following:

> My will to thee I sweetly surrender now,
> My will to God flame I ever bow,
> My will passing into thine
> I sweetly vow.

QUESTIONS & ANSWERS
with Elizabeth Clare Prophet on

Sexuality and Spirituality

SEX *and* LIFESTYLE

Q: **What do you think about unmarried couples living together? My boyfriend and I are living together. We're committed to each other and we expect to get married. Do you have any advice for us?**

A: For growth on the spiritual path, if a couple is committed to one another and plans to marry, I would recommend getting married rather than living together. Without the marriage commitment, when the inevitable challenges of a relationship come along, it may be easier to walk away rather than to work hard on the relationship. But when you have made the commitment and built trust and it is sealed in the marriage contract, you have a strong foundation that you can stand on together to meet whatever you may have to face.

When you're living together, if the relationship ends, then you carry the extra karmic patterns of this previous boyfriend or girlfriend. This weight can affect you in various ways, even if only subtly. And your connection with your Higher Self may be harder to maintain.

While you may share companionship and love when you're living together, you also share karma without the protection of the marriage blessing. However, when you pronounce your vows during the marriage ceremony, that vow becomes a blessing to each partner and, by the invocation given, the union is sealed and protected. Then you mutually bear one another's karma, and you are committed and take responsibility for that burden. You can grow in love and balance karma while you serve together to raise children or give to life in other ways.

Sometimes people avoid marriage because they don't want to carry the extra karma, the extra weight, the feeling of being restricted or confined. A deeply committed mutual relationship does require selflessness. Therefore, marriage is always sacrificial. If we see selfishness in ourselves, we can determine to become more selfless, more giving, more sacrificial. And marriage gives us this opportunity, which can offer great rewards.

Q: **If a couple is homosexual, can they raise the sacred fire and hold the light in their chakras, just as a married man and woman do?**

A: This is an important question for spiritual seekers who are striving to balance their chakras and raise the sacred fire. The answer lies in the understanding of the natural law of the polarization of male and female energies.

In the practice of the same-sex union, the energies of the sacred fire are lowered rather than raised. There is not the divine polarity and exchange of masculine and feminine energies that can occur between a man and a woman. In homosexual relations the exchange of energy between partners is in opposition. It's like putting two magnets of the same charge together— two positively charged ends or two negatively charged ends. By natural law, the like polarities oppose each other rather than naturally attract one another, as they do when the positive and negative charges are joined. A physical exchange between members of the same sex follows this same principle.

In homosexual practices, the balance of the feminine and masculine currents of the kundalini is lost. With each lifetime, whether we are male or female, we are given a certain charge of these kundalini currents at the base-of-the-spine chakra, which contains a male (alpha), or positive, current and a female (omega), or minus, current. If the homosexual person is male, he is misusing the masculine charge of the alpha current. Over time the masculine energy is depleted, contributing to the more effeminate nature of homosexual men. If the person is female, she is a misusing the feminine, omega, current. This misuse eventually deprives the woman of the fullness of the feminine potential, which causes a shift to a less intuitive state and to a coarser masculine energy. This is why the religions of the world teach that homosexuality is in opposition to the flow of the sacred fire in man and woman.

There is never any condemnation of anyone by God. This is simply the teaching that is based on the infinite wisdom of God and his caring for each soul on the homeward path. And while we do not judge anyone's free will choice, if people really understood the use of the sacred fire, they would do better. To engage in homosexual practices is to be at cross-purposes with oneself and with God's natural laws. And it becomes a setback to the soul's evolution.

Q: So if a person desires to change this lifestyle, do you think it's possible?

A: Many people say that one can abstain but one cannot change one's nature, but I don't agree. Change is always possible and it is the transcending message of heaven. It is simply a matter of changing the course of the river. When we habitually express a particular use of sexual energy, carving a specific pattern within ourself, energy tends to flow in that channel we have created. Homosexuality is something that has often continued from previous lifetimes and therefore these sexual tendencies may have been deeply established.

If a person truly desires to change the course of the river

and to create new channels for the flow of the energies of life, I would encourage him to fast and pray, to visualize those old riverbeds filled with the love of God and the violet flame, and to raise the sacred energies. Physical exercise and a change in social habits or associations will also be important. We must have patience with ourselves and with our evolving soul as we are working to close off one channel and open up another. It takes dedication and a great desire to overcome these habits, yet it is not a matter of guilt or condemnation. We are all children of light, beloved of God's heart, spiritually destined to reclaim the fullness of our divine nature.

SEX *and* DATING

Q: **Do you think it's a good idea for a couple to have sexual intercourse before marriage so they can determine if they're compatible in this way?**

A: I don't find any basis for the idea that "Well, we're going to try it out and see if we're suited." I feel that there's probably nothing more natural to the human race than the correct expression of sex when misuses aren't involved. The natural flow of sex is something that nobody has to be taught. If you love on a spiritual level and you share things in common and have found your true love because you have been willing to wait—you've been willing to lead the celibate life and concentrate the energies of the sacred fire within yourself—then you have everything right at all levels and all of your energies will mesh properly. And sex, which is just an expression of everything else, will also be right.

Q: **What do you think about physical intimacy while people are dating?**

A: You have to gauge this by your own self-mastery. It's important to understand that even though a relationship may be wholly pure, physical contact begins the flow of energy to sexual fulfillment. And once the spiral is begun, it's sometimes difficult to turn it back.

I once read a very interesting article by a psychologist in which he said that the moment the sex interplay begins you go from hand-holding to petting to the complete sexual act. Each time you come together with the opposite sex, it requires more and more contact for a certain level of fulfillment because of the buildup of energy. So with adolescents, for instance, there's a certain balance of the masculine-feminine energies that occurs with hand-holding. Then that becomes not enough, and then it's the next stage and the next, and so on.

For an adult, if you've been married before, if you've lived with someone before, if you've had sexual relations, it often requires very little stimulus for you to require sexual intercourse because your body is used to the energy flow at that level. And therefore it's for the older couples or the ones who have experienced this before that greater discipline is usually required to keep the energies raised.

You might decide, then, it isn't worth getting one's energies primed for sexual intercourse. While you're dating you can raise your sacred energies through physical activities, like hiking, mountain climbing, swimming, and so forth. You can do things together that uplift your energies. You can spend time together, get to know each other, share in nature, talk about God, and not get your chakras so involved in physical intimacy. People who have taken my advice on this have been the happiest and have brought the greatest purity to a marriage.

It's a question of how you want to use your energies and how much mastery you have. Most people who get married have some residue of misqualified energy in the lower chakras that they are going to have to transmute in their relationship. So before you marry, you can also spend time purifying the chakras of misuses of the sacred fire from previous relationships so that those desires and habits do not impinge upon your new relationship.

MARRIAGE *and* SEXUALITY

Q: Can I be married and still lead a spiritual life?

A: In the East, in India for example, it is understood by Hindus and Buddhists that it is perfectly natural to have different phases of one's life. When the couple is of childbearing age, it is the natural time to bring forth children if this is desired. Later in life, when those years have been fulfilled, the husband and wife may elect to live a more celibate life.

Both aspects of life are considered wholly natural for the fulfillment of the soul. Both are needed and allowed; one is holy and the other is holy. It is a question of steps along the spiritual path. They are both rituals that can take place within the natural order of the cycles of life. And that is what ritual is for—for the ordering of our lives so we know what to expect of God and of ourselves each step of the way.

Q: Is it possible to raise the kundalini and also gain energy while I'm married and sexually active with my wife? Or is it necessarily a diminishing of energy?

A: Depending on the level of attainment of both people and many factors that are involved, including the frequency of sexual relations, there may not be a considerable loss. In the sexual union, the gain of sharing love and the balancing of energies can be beneficial for both.

For some people on the spiritual path, the bliss and the gains experienced through raising the light are so great that the interchange in a sexual relationship naturally diminishes. It may become less frequent. However, the sexual interchange may still be a natural part of your marriage and necessary for balancing energies.

A determining factor on how much sex one should have is to recognize when an excess costs too much in terms of other creativity. It's always about finding your point of balance.

So you have to agree together about how often you're going to have sexual relations because both partners have needs. Since part of being married is a commitment to consider each other, you have to be mindful of the desires of your partner.

The ideal situation is for you and your spouse to have the support, the strength, and the love of each other at the same time that you choose to pursue a spiritual path together. Together as a team you can decide to fast together, to pray together, to be celibate together, to have children together. You can have the best of both worlds.

Q: I have a new job where I will be traveling and away from my wife, so I have some concerns about what will happen to our sexual relationship. Do you have any advice for us?

A: If you are entering a life of serving others, teaching, or other professional work and you are separated from each other for periods of time, I would view this as a good challenge for your mastery of these energies. This can be healthy for both of you because it gives you the sense that you can be complete in yourself. You can find fulfillment by raising the light and merging with God while you are apart.

PART FOUR

MARRIAGE
and the
SPIRITUAL PATH

The marriage of a man and woman
is meant to be mystical,
a commemoration of the soul's reunion
with God through the Higher Self.

CHAPTER 9

MARRIAGE:
A SOUL PERSPECTIVE

*M*arriage is the most sacred union upon earth. It commemorates the union of twin flames and the union of the soul with her God Presence. So marriage reflects the soul's ultimate experience of wholeness, and thus it is mystical and holy. Within marriage the husband and wife have the opportunity to develop wholeness individually and together as a unit.

As each one in the marriage serves, nurtures, and loves the soul of the other, this wholeness increases. It can be an ever-expanding love that blesses not only themselves but also many others. In giving that love, the husband and wife are also loving God and drawing down his energy. They are putting on more of God's consciousness by becoming that which they perceive of God in each other. Therefore that love is a magnet that enables both to become more of God. In this way marriage provides an opportunity for spiritual development.

As the marriage partners draw down more of God's energy, they have a greater ability to fulfill their mission, to help others, and to balance karmic debts, especially through the reciprocity of family relationships. A purpose, goal, or dream that the husband and wife forge together can greatly enhance a successful and joyful marriage. It can override the elements of karma, the opposition to the union, the discord, and the petty things that come up in day-to-day living. Without this united vision, the marriage may not last. But with this vision, both souls can be propelled to their highest fulfillment in life.

FRIENDSHIP *and* FOUNDATIONS *of* MARRIAGE

How do you really know if someone is meant to be your future spouse? As a friendship becomes a more serious relationship, you can be doing things together that are normal, everyday activities, not just idealized situations like going out for dinner and arranging dates that are fun. It's important to observe how your friend handles all types of ordinary life circumstances, such as dealing with daily stress, taking care of finances, interacting with others, keeping a home, and holding a job. You can also see what he does with his spare time.

This would be a time for discussing your relationship, your likes and dislikes, whether you see a foundation for the future, and so forth. You will want to observe how your friend relates to conflict and deeply personal issues. As the relationship progresses, it can be a good time to study relationship books and reflect on how the concepts apply to yourself and the relationship.[1]

You can support each other in schooling and careers. This encourages each person's individual growth and allows both people to explore their interests, inclinations and talents. A tried-and-true friendship that blossomed under extraordinary circumstances was the basis of this couple's strong marriage:

> *When I was a young woman, I had several serious relationships but they did not work out. I decided that I*

*was done with dating for a while and was going to con-
centrate on my own wholeness. One evening I was sitting
in my favorite green armchair with a book and could feel
acute pain in my heart. I meditated on this and realized it
was loneliness for a mate. I cried out to God, "I'm never
going to marry. I never want to have anything to do with
men again!" Shortly after my impassioned cry, I heard a
calm voice, the inner voice, or "the voice" in my heart, say
to me, "But what if you met a man whom you could
marry? What are the qualities you would want him to
have?" I had never thought about this before.*

*I got out a piece of paper and wrote down the specific
characteristics I wanted in a mate as well as the kind of
lifestyle I wanted for us. There were twenty-three items on
the list when I was finished. After I wrote the list, I realized that if I wanted to attract this kind of man, I needed
to develop these qualities myself, and I began working on
it. I kept this list with me for years.*

*More than two years later, after doing this ritual,
I met my future husband at a social event. He seemed
loud, overly self-confident, and walked with a swagger.
I was repelled by him. He had holes in his jeans, a beer
belly, shoulder length red-gold curls, and chewed on a
pipe. Charismatic and popular with many, all sorts of
women were drawn to him. And I was not his type, being
deeply spiritual, quiet, intense and careful in my dress. My
friend came up to me at the event and said, "Oh, you've
already met! This is the man I was bringing you to see."*

*About three months later, we went out to dinner on
our first date and, as life would unfold, the next day
I became very sick with a brain infection and was in the
hospital three times over the next few months and almost
died. This man, who hardly knew me, was by my side*

*daily, cooking me soup, paying my rent and doctor bills,
and asking for nothing in return. In our talks during the
year that I was very ill, we spoke deeply and frequently.
We became the dearest of friends.*

*While he was rough around the edges, he was the
man with the heart and the practical qualities I had listed
years ago. And his love and care restored my life. We did
eventually marry. Since we met forty years ago, we have
gone through many karmic periods. Yet through thick and
thin, he has been my truest helpmate and companion, my
precious love and loyal friend in times of serious illness,
raising our children, and in our mutual service and passion
to educate children.*

THE MARRIAGE DECISION

Often, especially when we're young, we don't fully understand
the significance of marriage. Consequently, some of us rush into marriage without considering the ramifications. Without realizing it consciously, we may be running away from problems in our life, hoping
that marriage will resolve them. We may be immature when we marry,
and then a number of years later we may realize that it wasn't the
best step. Or we might believe that marriage is out of style, so living
together becomes a way of life. So it is helpful to realistically consider the decision to marry.

When people want to know whether or not they should get
married, I ask them two questions. First, "Have you considered if
your individual service to life would be enhanced, enriched, and
greater in marriage than it would be separately?" One plus one always equals three, because there are three in the marriage union—
you and your spouse and the Spirit of God, the omnipresence of
God. With this union, every phase of marriage is sacred. The second
question I ask is, "Are you deeply in love? Do you have a fire burn-

ing deep in your heart, the fire that can commemorate your love for God?"

If you can answer these two questions but you are still hesitant, I suggest that you wait. Don't move until "an elephant steps on your foot." When you are sure that it's right, then you're ready to seal your love in marriage.

When love is true and real and when it is a whirling fire in your heart, nothing can overcome it, not even your own subconscious or psychology. Nothing can overcome such love because it is the greatest power in the universe. This love may begin as a spark, as a candle flame that you can nurture and expand. It is a flame that holds the potential of a blazing sun. Without this intense love, it can be difficult to overcome adversity.

Therefore marriage has two requirements: a greater service to God, greater than you can render alone, and an intense fiery love. The affirmation of these essential qualities provides the foundation for a strong and productive marriage.

PREPARING *for* MARRIAGE

When you are about to get married, you and your fiancé are filled with love and with an exciting vision and hope for the future. This new beginning can be one of the most exciting times of your life. With a desire to be together for the rest of your life, practical steps can be taken to assure that the marriage is built on a solid foundation. Since marriage is also a contract, a contract of love, it's important for both people to agree on the stipulations of that contract. What does your partner expect in marriage? What does he expect to receive? What does he expect to give? And what about you? While having a contract may not sound very spiritual, having the clarity of expectations creates a strong chalice for the love shared in marriage.

The key to forming this contract is communication. You can

meet with your spouse to talk over and agree upon the conditions of the contract. You'll probably want to discuss key issues, like how you will handle money and your sexual relationship as well as your daily work schedule, your needs for time off, privacy, and independence. Whether or not you want to have children, how many, and other personal family concerns are also essential topics to explore. As long as both people know and are clear about what to expect, you have the basis for a contract.

Before and after marriage, one of the most important factors for a strong relationship is keeping the lines of communication open. Marriage is a process of giving and receiving and it's important to let one another know each other's needs at all levels. It's important to make these needs clear in words rather than in moods, silence, or aloofness. The relationship will benefit by openness, trust, and honor so that when you share, you are not feeling threatened that you will be hurt or the other person will be offended. In this way, each person is respected, understood, and considered. When you are preparing for marriage, establishing and building such communication will serve you well.

THE CEREMONY *and the* SEALING

If we accept marriage as a sacrament, as a sacred union of souls, then the marriage ceremony allows God to be a part of the marriage from its inception. The marriage ceremony given through a minister, priest, rabbi, or another representative authorized to perform this ceremony is a gift from God. In this ceremony the marriage is sealed by the invocation of the marriage blessing. Whether or not the spiritual representative performing the ceremony is considered worthy, we go before a representative of God, before his Higher Self. Through the invocation, the human institution of marriage becomes blessed and sanctified.

Until you pronounce your vows at the altar of marriage, you don't enter into the true marriage contract in the sense of bearing and transmuting one another's karma. Marriage requires this contract and commitment as you walk together through karmic cycles and grow together on the spiritual path.

As previously mentioned, the marriage ceremony protects the exchange of energies in sexual union. It provides a sealing, as a circle of energy, a sphere of white light, around both souls for the protection of the sacred fire. The blessing of God consecrates the sacred fire and its exchange between you and your spouse.

A SACRED UNION

Thus the marriage relationship between man and woman is a sacred union because the polarity of the marriage partners always represents the Father and Mother aspects of God. You can look at your spouse as God in manifestation, and therefore you can love that one with the highest love that you would have for God and for your twin flame. In that respect, it doesn't matter if you are married to your twin flame or if you have ever met your twin flame. You can love with your whole heart, and this love can be transforming, even liberating.

In coming to know your wife or husband, you also put on aspects of their consciousness. This is evident in people who have been married for many years. They begin to look alike, act alike, think alike. In a sense, marriage is a process by which the man assimilates aspects of the divine feminine from his wife, while the woman assimilates aspects of the divine masculine from her husband. It is a spiritual opportunity whereby you strive to become the androgynous whole. Ideally, at any given moment, if you stand apart as two individuals, each one of you will contain the wholeness of the other.

LIKE TWO TALL PINES STANDING FIRM

The opposite of this wholeness is possessiveness and dependence. Instead of being like two pine trees standing tall and firm, this is like two sticks leaning against one another. When one is removed, the other falls over. This dependence can weaken a marriage. We can love God in our husband or in our wife, but this is not to say, "My husband is my God" or "My wife is my God."

We cannot expect a marriage to supply the answers to all of life's problems. We might wish that in marriage somehow all the pain and sorrow of life will be eliminated and all of our greatest longings—including our dreams, fantasies, and subconscious desires—will be fulfilled. But this is not the case. It is one of those illusions that society portrays.

If we are dependent or possessive, we may put unrealistic demands and strains on our marriage partner. The wife expects all of these fulfillments in the husband, the husband expects all of these fulfillments in the wife, and the gods themselves could not possibly live up to all the ideals that we have concerning the supreme bliss of the married state. These demands can stretch a marriage to the breaking point because the partners are demanding what marriage is not intended to give.

But when both people provide the qualities and strengths that they want in their partner, it contributes to a stronger and healthier marriage. It is a complementary relationship. Each one expects to be the pillar in that marriage, and what comes back from the other person is not because of a level of expectation but rather as a grace and as an added gift. It is most supportive of the marriage for one's expectations to be not of one's mate but rather of oneself—an expectation, indeed a desire, to give the gift of the best of oneself, one's Higher Self.

And you know what happens then? You are totally free to give. You don't just give because someone is nice to you. You give because there is a fountain of love overflowing within you.

WHAT HAPPENED *to the* HONEYMOON?

Before a couple marries, usually they see everything that is good, beautiful, and wonderful about each other. It's the attainment of the partner that stands out. This is a sweet interval and a time of grace.

Sometime after the couple marries, they wake up one morning and, as they say, the honeymoon is over. Each one senses an extra burden, an extra pack on their back. The wife is carrying the husband's karma and the husband is carrying the wife's karma. This can be unsettling. It's like putting on someone else's shoes. They're not quite comfortable, they're not quite worn in the right places, and they don't even fit. So sometimes people start resenting this extra burden that they have taken on in their marriage, but this is part of the marriage agreement.

When you take the vow "for better or for worse, for richer or for poorer, in sickness and in health," each one of you is taking a vow to share the karma of the other, and it becomes a joint load. On the positive side, the weaknesses of your spouse can be balanced by your strengths, and your weaknesses can be balanced by your spouse's strengths, and this is one of the purposes of marriage. In this way the husband and wife complement each other, learning and growing together.

Marriage is an exercise in being the partner to your twin flame. The fact that karma is being shared highlights the reality that marriage has a purpose, a spiritual purpose. Marriage provides a divine unit to balance your karma while drawing forth the attainment of your good karma in service to God and humanity. In this way the positive karma from your past lives strengthens your marriage, adding vibrancy and vision to your union. Together, your positive karma can magnetize joyful service, inspirations, children, or other manifestations of your shared spiritual attainment.

As karmic cycles unfold and you face sickness or hardship, you realize that this is what you have agreed to share. You may experience the beauties and the joys of marriage, but you also may share in the unwinding of karma as it comes to you throughout life.

Thus you have a choice. You can allow your karma to take over your lives and burden the marriage, or you can change it. When you understand that your karma can blind you to the virtues of your partner and can cause negative feelings to fester, you can make a deliberate choice to transmute that karma and to spiritualize your marriage. Each morning at dawn you have the release of the karma you must deal with that day. If you transmute it together, you can go forward in creativity throughout the day. You can make the most of your sharing.

THE BALANCE *in* GIVING

During your marriage you may find that the challenges are great and you may not be prepared for them. Meeting these challenges takes understanding, support, and love. Divine love always has met and always will meet every human need, but each person has to embody that divine love.

One of the ways that love is demonstrated is through givingness. A marriage is built on what each partner decides to give to the other. To realize the greatest benefit from marriage, each one's giving needs to be in balance. If you give too much, you have nothing left of yourself and this is a false sacrifice whereby you may lose your self-mastery or your integrity. If you have to give love and support over and over again to the point where you are compromising important aspects of yourself or your life, even your mission and your goal in life, then your marriage may not be sustainable.

Instead of giving too much, one partner may withhold giving. This might be demonstrated as selfishness, a sense of aloofness, or a holier-than-thou attitude, for instance, when one partner assumes that he is better than his spouse.

When husbands and wives are giving in a balanced way, they

approach their spouse with the attitude: "What can I give? What can I do for my spouse? What can I do for our children?" It is the same reason that the soul goes to God—not to get but to give. We go to God to love him. The love that is returned is a blessing, but it is secondary. It is the same in the marriage relationship.

LOVING *the* SOUL *in the* STATE *of* BECOMING WHOLE

Marriage calls for a couple to continually grow in love. It is a love of forgiveness, compassion, and understanding. It is a willingness to pick up the pieces and start over again when there are problems, when there is discord, when there are challenges. It is a determination to keep on trying, to keep on loving, to keep on forgiving, to keep on nourishing the soul of one another, to keep on identifying one's husband or wife as an aspect of God that requires ministration and utter devotion.

This does not mean tolerance of bad habits or a disregard of unkind actions. It's the fine line of loving the soul that is in the state of becoming whole. It is also not the pious, self-righteous attitude of "I love your Higher Self but don't get in my way with your human personality. I won't stand for it." That is not the point.

The point of understanding and love is the realization that the soul is in the state of becoming one with her Higher Self. It is, in a sense, the reality of each individual here and now. It's what we love in one another. We have to be willing to keep working with that soul, walking with that soul, praying for that soul, and loving that soul. Each individual is like a flower, and that flower has to be free to unfold in its own time, in its own way. And in marriage you discover the ways that the fragrance of your individual flowers blend, how your soul-patterns blend.

Mark taught me that when I'm counseling those who are married I should tell them how sacred is the love of husband and wife and that it is the very love of the Father-Mother God. This love begins at home. Choose love and you will prosper and all will go well. Choose the hallowed circle of the Father-Mother God and find succor from the crassness of the world and surcease from all struggle.

This couple shares two practical rituals that have helped them on their journey of love.

Throughout our marriage of many years, I have been aware of the fabric of our marriage and the weaving of this fabric through harmony. And so I didn't want to "rip it" by inharmony or by saying things too emotionally. We have had a few rituals that have really helped us, especially in the first seven years of our marriage.

Puppet shows were a creative and effective way for us to talk through our difficulties. I used a little elephant puppet and a little girl puppet named Emily that my husband bought me. I would have the puppets act out the arguments and feelings of fear or worry. Our puppet shows externalized the issues and took them out of the realm of confrontation. My husband would watch my show with a sort of amused, charmed, and concerned look, and usually he didn't say anything or get defensive. It was a successful way to communicate without fighting, accusing, or manipulating.

We also had a ritual of setting a time to meet about every two months to discuss the bedrock, painful issues, such as alcohol, smoking, money, personal growth, or raising our children. These meetings were not about the daily things. On a day-to-day basis we spent time sharing, laughing, and emphasizing the positive; I didn't nag or focus on the negatives. On the other hand, in our regular bimonthly meetings the really difficult issues were confronted in as diplomatic a fashion as we could manage. We

The Creation of Twin Flames — Plate 1*a*

The Creation of Twin Flames — Plate 1*b*

Plate 2a   The Creation of Twin Flames

Plate 2b   The Creation of Twin Flames

Plate 3

Plate 4   Archangel Michael

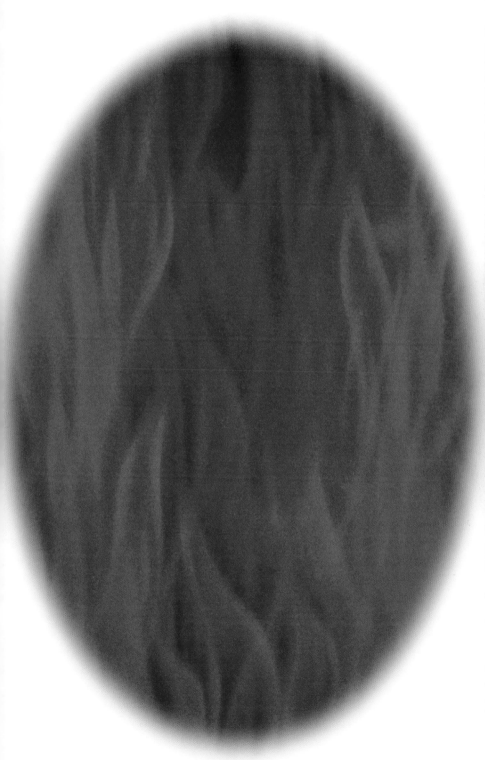

The Violet Flame

Plate 5

Plate 6

The Seven Major Chakras

Kuan Yin, Representative of the Divine Mother in the East   Plate 7

Plate 8

Mary, Representative of the Divine Mother in the West

*didn't argue. Often tears were shed. We would each com-
mit to working on things to do for the next meeting in two
months.*

*Afterwards we would go for a walk, watch the sunset
over the ocean, or go out to dinner, and we would feel our
love triumph over the pain. Our marriage has flourished
by allowing this space to work on our marriage—our walk
of love.*

FLEXIBILITY *in the* FLOW *of* LOVE— MARRIAGE ROLES

Marriage is like two intertwining flames. When you look into
a physical fire, you see that you can never capture the flame and say,
"This is the shape of the flame." It never has a shape; it keeps moving. The two flames in a marriage are constantly leaping, moving,
and taking on different characteristics of God.

Since they are two flames, they can be blending in harmony.
When one takes a shape, the other molds itself around that shape.
This is the day-to-day creativity and flow of love that can exist be-
tween a husband and wife.

This flexibility in the flow of love is demonstrated in the interplay of the various roles in the marriage relationship. In other words,
the wife is not always wife. She is every aspect of the feminine nature
of God at one time or another—mother, daughter, sister, wife. She
may be the child or she may be the mature matriarch. Similarly, the
husband need not play the rigid role of husband, because God is not
in the rigid role of husband. God appears to us as father, son, brother,
neighbor, friend.

These different roles give an expansive nature to the marriage
relationship. When we have this flexibility, this movement of the
flow of love, we can enjoy one another as friends when we want to
be friends. We can enjoy one another as confidants, as partners in a

joint endeavor. We can enjoy one another as parents. We can enjoy one another in almost any capacity.

Most important in sharing roles in the marriage relationship is that when one partner is having difficulties, the identity of the spouse is so strong that he or she becomes a rock of the Real Self, the Higher Self, holding firm while the other one is struggling. The spouse can hold the sure vision of the marriage, seeing that partner through the difficulty with a steady love.

But just as matter itself requires a rest—your shoes need a rest, machinery needs a rest—so we also need a rest from certain roles. We all know that there are moments when the mother has wisdom and understanding. But sometimes she may want to step aside and be, for instance, like a sister with understanding and a listening ear or like a child with a spontaneous exuberance. We know that there are moments when being the protector and master of the home is a heavy burden. So the husband may take the role of son or brother or fellow pilgrim on the path of life, and this can be a necessary relief.

If we are always demanding that our spouse be the epitome of our concept of what we think a husband or a wife should be, we're going to be sadly disappointed, because nobody fits rigidly into one role. And if we make our relationship rigid, based on what society tells us marriage should be, we lose out on the richness and the depth that God has given us to experience.

I remember counseling a woman a long time ago who could not get along with her husband. I said to her, "Don't you understand that all of us at some time need a mother and we all need to provide that role? Sometimes you have to be mother even to your husband and sometimes he has to be father to you." Well, to her this was outrageous! She absolutely was not going to accept the role of mother in relation to her husband.

When this happens, we miss the important understanding that somewhere deep down in the soul we are all little children. We have that tender spot that can still be hurt and still reacts as a child. We can identify this in ourself and we can understand it. But perhaps when we look at someone else, we cancel it out. We say, "No, he's an adult. He should behave like an adult. He shouldn't be making demands on me that a child would make on a parent." We lose a great opportunity when we deny any adult the right to be a child at times. Everyone has the right to be a child sometimes.

Every now and then, a husband needs to be the one who takes care and nurtures. And the wife may need to be the support and provider. This flexibility can provide a great strength and mutuality in giving, as the couple below experienced with one another.

> *In our marriage, we have experienced many challenges (as in most marriages)—serious illnesses, medical surgeries, loss of work, sudden moves, tragic accidents, and death. Some challenges have been jolting and some more gradual. Through thick and thin, my wife and I have stood lovingly and loyally by each other. I remember sitting for hours during my wife's major surgery, being by her side when she woke up, and caring for her during the weeks afterwards. When I had a sudden job loss, she increased her work hours and was the major breadwinner. Many times we have loved and sacrificed for each other with hardly a discussion because we share such a deep and abiding trust.*

In a strong and healthy marriage, masculine and feminine spiritual roles are constantly changing. It's a tai chi relationship where from moment to moment one is dominant and the other is supportive, and these roles switch back and forth in the dynamic rhythm and interchange of the polarities of life. When you are equally mature and equally desirous of making a relationship work, the quality of deferring to one's partner so that that one might be dominant is just part of the giving process of a relationship.

If two people are united in marriage, at times one of them may need to surrender. My husband Mark would step back and let me do what I needed to do, and then at other times I would step back. It was a great balance. This is like a cosmic dance. It isn't that one suppresses the other, but it is the self-sacrificing aspect of every relationship.

I know that Mark sacrificed greatly for me, and he sometimes expressed the feminine qualities that I saw as my role. He taught me and he had no greater joy than when he could bring me forward.

In her spiritual role of carrying the feminine polarity, one of woman's most fundamental inner needs is to support others, to give of herself completely. Many women can find this in a life of service. Marriage provides an opportunity for woman to lovingly serve so that the talents and gifts of her husband and children can flourish. No matter what seems to be going on outwardly in a marriage, for many women it is essential for them to experience this givingness at a deep inner level in order to feel fulfilled.

The man in a marriage has a similar initiation, or challenge, of the masculine polarity. A man's sacrifice is his labor, his work for providing and caring for his wife and children. A man must be free to create and to forge his destiny. Unless he integrates his will, his mind, and his heart for that labor, which he brings symbolically as the bouquet of flowers for his wife, he will not be totally fulfilled in the marriage.

KARMIC MARRIAGES

None of us fully know what we are getting into when we start a relationship or a marriage. People grow, and cycle by cycle through the years karma is outplayed. Things we did not see in our partner at first may surface later, or the chemistry of the relationship may bring out situations that one never suspected. So sometimes marriages that are karmic are brief and sometimes they last a lifetime.

If a couple has difficult karma from previous lifetimes, as long as that karma remains it is binding unless they have an alternative means for working it out. In these cases, marriage provides the crucible and the intensity of love and service necessary for balancing the karma, especially when it involves raising children and caring for a family.

When we realize that we are in such a relationship, perhaps seeing that this person is not our twin flame, it is not lawful to then treat that relationship halfheartedly or even resentfully and not give it the best and most fervent love of our heart. It could be as if one would say, "Well, this person is not my twin flame. This is just a karmic situation, so I'll give it a token effort and bide my time until the real thing comes along." That is a very good way to prolong the resolution of karma and to make more karma.

If you want to know whether yours is a karmic marriage or one of twin flames, it can help to go within your heart, meditate, pray, and give your decrees with fervor to purify your consciousness. Give yourself time to transcend your current level of awareness so that you can receive a clear understanding of the nature of your relationship. When you come up higher, you may get the perspective of whether or not it is a karmic marriage.

If both people in a karmic marriage strive together, they can grow in love and service, as the following couple did.

It was my wedding day. My future husband and I were deeply in love. I was sure of our union, yet at a profound level there was still some confusion in my soul. Truly I loved him, and yet for the previous year I had experienced times of nonclarity. How was I to know if this was truly the right person? What if the marriage got hard and I needed to get out? Am I really in love or do I just want to be married? Would we live happily ever after? So many questions and no satisfactory answers.

The main doors to the church opened. I could see my fiancé standing nervously at the altar rail. My dad tugged on my arm. I couldn't move—so much whirling around inside of me. What if, what if, what if?

Dad leaned over and whispered in my ear that it was time to go, and he pinched me on the tender inside of my arm. Just being my dad, he thought this was all humorous and quite normal. His joy broke my cycle of fear and down the aisle we went.

Did we live happily ever after? Yes and no. It has been a karmic marriage, with cycles of great happiness and fulfillment and cycles of unmitigated challenges. After many years, the ebb and flow of the returning karma taught us to determine what the priorities of our lives would be. We had to decide if we could support each other by giving more and loving more deeply. And, most importantly, we needed to discern if we could grow spiritually and become more of our true selves through the process.

We've learned how to nurture our marriage with a whole lot more give-and-take, times of family fun, travel, community service, and a strong commitment to a spiritual path. In addition, after long and truthful discussions and lots of prayer, we have chosen to remain together to raise our children and to trust in God to guide us through the rough spots, which surface less and less each year.

Looking back on our many years of marriage, it is clear that long and truthful discussions were repeated many times and the commitment to each other renewed yet again. We've learned how to be honest, to stick with discomfort until we get to resolution, and to come out on the other end stronger and more peaceful. We've learned that the investment in our spiritual lives and support for each other's growth during times of change is part of every worthwhile relationship.

Over time, as our karma resolves, we observe how

*love and joyfulness increase, and so we continue to pray
and work towards living "happily forever after." Our circle
of love grows and expands through our children and
grandchildren, our friends, and our dedication to several
community service endeavors. Our hearts tell us that for
us it has been well worth the work.*

DIVORCE—
STAYING TOGETHER *or* PARTING WAYS

Social problems in modern-day life are impacting the strength
of the marriage union. The symptoms of the besieged family are
rampant—teenage pregnancy, economic challenges, rising crime and
drug abuse, child and spouse abuse. The state of marriage is being
compromised and it is in peril. Divorce rates are high. Some marriages are cold and brittle, and children are brought forth in this
environment. Some children grow up without the love that should
have been imparted to them by their fathers and mothers.

Compounding the social pressures on marriage are the added
personal issues. When you are married and have a family, your life
is no longer your own. The husband and wife both need to be constantly serving, constantly giving, and also sacrificing for the benefit
of the family. Though there are many good reasons for divorce, the
ending of a marriage is often caused because the partners, who may
be well suited for one another, are not willing to sacrifice individually for the good of the family. If one of them stops giving, the marriage may be in jeopardy. In addition, since some people can tend to
be selfish and to expect too much from their mates, they may feel
that if everything is not perfect in a marriage, it should be dissolved.

In some situations divorce is appropriate, while at other times
it may not be the best course of action. Sometimes people divorce
because they are not willing to examine and take accountability for
their own reactions. For instance, people may have condemnation

toward their spouse or a sense of resentment. They may have a lack of tolerance because their spouse practices a different religion than they do. Or maybe their partner has different interests, different likes and dislikes, and this becomes a point of unhappiness or conflict. In reality, marriage is naturally a blend of similarities and differences, and if both spouses are too much the same, the marriage could become dull and boring.

Not too long ago, I received a phone call from a young woman who was seriously devoted to her religion, but she was married to a man who had no interest in it. Furthermore, he didn't like her religious practices or the amount of time she spent on them.

This woman called me and said, "We've been separated for two weeks now. I feel so ashamed that I have a husband who doesn't have the same beliefs that I do. I think we're going to split up, but I had to talk to you first. What should I do?"

So I said to her, "First of all, a marriage cannot endure unless you love one another with your whole heart. Do you love him?" "Yes." "Does he love you?" "Yes." "Then why are you splitting up?" "Well, he doesn't believe what I believe." I said, "What are you worried about? That's not your problem; that's God's problem. Is he a good husband?" "Yes." "Is he a provider, a protector?" "Yes, he's a perfect husband."

The question is not what your spouse believes. Someone can be a living example of a kind and trustworthy person without consciously understanding a spiritual path. Watch the person you are married to. Is he loving? Is he living an honorable life? Is he a good man? Does he fulfill the marriage covenant, the marriage role? Does he respect you? Do you love him? If all of this is yes, then leave his spiritual training to God.

It is important for spouses to respect each other's right to their own religious beliefs. If your spouse has a different religion, ask where he or she would like to go to church. Then go to that church together. If your husband wants to worship God in the hills, then take a hike with him on Sunday morning and pray in the hills. It is what you are that counts; it is the light and love that counts.

So I said to the woman who called, "Do you ever go to church with your husband?" "No." I said, "What are you doing on Sunday morning?" "Well, I go to my church." "What time does it start?" "Well, it starts around eleven." I said, "Can't you find a church of your husband's choice that you can attend with him at nine?" "Why, I never thought of that."

As I talked to her about the situation, she told me that her husband had come over after two weeks and was playing with their little son in the living room. She talked about how much he adored that child and how it would be just terrible if they were separated. I said, "Yes, that would be terrible. You should go back and tell your husband how much you appreciate him, how wonderful he is, how good he is to you, how grateful you are that he's the father of your child, and that you want to support him." She was overjoyed.

Marriage takes compassion for one another and it does take work. But what is most important is harmony. If there are children in the family, it is essential that they see a unity of the parents, a proper and dignified representation of the Father-Mother God, and not continual strife and degradation of oneself or one's partner. If there is constant and considerable inharmony between a husband and wife, they may be making more karma together than they would if they were apart. In such a case it might be lawful for the couple to consider parting ways.

If a marriage isn't working, the couple may come to realize that its purpose has been fulfilled and they may have other concerns and callings to tend to and goals to accomplish. Each one will need to do a lot of soul-searching to come to that conclusion. And if children are involved, of course it is more difficult.

To stay married for the sake of staying married is not reason enough to maintain that arrangement, just as love for the sake of loving a human personality or sex for the sake of sex is not enough reason to maintain those relationships. We all make mistakes, so if at some point you feel that the marriage was a mistake, it does not need to bind you for a whole lifetime. Perhaps when you got married you didn't fully realize the significance of it or what it would entail, or maybe you grew in separate directions from your spouse over time.

You may come to the place in life where regardless of what anybody else thinks or does or wants or needs, you realize that you are not being fulfilled and you are not adding either to your inner spiritual stature or to that of your spouse. If you don't do something about the inner gnawing, longing, and pulling in your life that you feel, nobody is going to win. And even though the person you are married to may think that the marriage is fine, the marriage may indeed be stopping that person's progress as well as your own.

Ultimately, we have to make selfless decisions, but we also have to make selfish decisions. What I mean by selfish is that if we don't preserve ourselves for another day of giving, we may find that we, along with the universe, are going to be the loser.

Divorce just might be the best step for both parties to take in a given situation in their lives. We can look at the purpose of a relationship from the sense of the soul going through an experience, a learning process, or paying off a karmic debt. When people have worked at their marriage but still sense that the purpose of the marriage has been fulfilled, then they don't need to feel obligated to perpetuate a relationship that is either without purpose or has become negative.

Understandably, it may be difficult to know when our karma is balanced. We can owe someone so much karma that by the time we are finished paying that karma, we have such a habit of being with that person that the habit carries on when the karma is over, and so we remain with our spouse.

If a couple decides to divorce, I recommend waiting at least two years before remarrying. This allows the individuals to work on their psychology, transmute their karma, and bring themselves to a higher place in consciousness in order to attract the perfect spouse.

THE LOVING UNION *of* MARRIAGE *and* FAMILY

Enfolded in the sacred relationship of marriage, the family provides the foundation for love's creativity and expansion. For the true function of the family is to create a hallowed circle of life with love at its heart. In fact, the family is the basic unit of divine love on earth. The love between a man and a woman forms a circle of love that widens, as selflessness also widens, to include first the offspring and then the community and then the whole world in that circle of love. That unit of love is the shock absorber for all who abide in the family. It is a unit of balance and wholeness as a man and woman honor their vows of love together and gain self-mastery.

The definition of *family* is father and mother in loving union: *f-a-m-i-l-y*—*f* = father, *m* = mother, *i* = in, *l* = loving, *y* = union. Ultimately, its purpose is for man and woman to work as one in service of the Higher Self in all. So the family is the cradle for bringing forth the Higher Self in father, in mother, and in their offspring. It is the birthplace not only for incoming souls but also for the creative genius of new ideas, projects, or world service.

The family is the place of opportunity for souls to share positive karma and balance negative karma. Sometimes a child is assigned by God to a family because one or both parents have good karma with the soul of that child. Sometimes it's because something from past lives needs to be resolved between the parents and the child or between the child and his siblings. And sometimes it's a little of both—a little good karma and a little nonresolution. Through day-to-day interactions of family members, rough spots are uncovered and there is opportunity to practice forgiveness, tolerance, and love.

The souls in families can come together through adoption also. Chance plays no part in adoption. The soul of an adopted child can be the same soul that a couple would otherwise conceive biologi-cally. Sometimes it is the karma of one or both of the biological parents to give birth to a child so that through adoption the child can get to his God-ordained parents, who may not be able to have children. If the birth of that child is not a necessity of karma, it is a service that the biological parents can perform to enable that soul to fulfill her mission with her God-ordained family.

Regardless of whether the parents are biological or adoptive, families are brought together to learn lessons, balance karma, enhance love, and serve together. The spiritual life of the parents can bring protection, strength, and harmony to the family. Loving care and heartfelt prayers that the mother and father offer on behalf of their children are some of the deepest joys of raising a family.

CHAPTER 10

THE MARRIAGE RITUAL

*W*hether it's the union of twin flames, soul mates, or karmic partners, the marriage of a man and woman is meant to be mystical, a commemoration of the soul's reunion with God through the Higher Self. God has ordained the celebration of this union on earth in the marriage ritual, the sexual union between husband and wife. This celebration of the sacred union is for the procreation of life, for life begetting life, for the expansion of love.

The interchange of divine love in the marriage relationship is meant to be the same creative love that framed the universe in the beginning, when God as Father gave forth the command, "Let there be light," and God as Mother answered, "And there was light."[1] This creative flow can be expressed not only in the physical union but also, if the couple chooses, during cycles of dedicated celibacy when each partner goes within to commune with God.

The release of the energies of the sacred fire in sexual union is probably the most intense experience that we know of in this physical plane. It is a release of a great amount of energy—physically as well as spiritually. Therefore, God has given us the sacrament of marriage and the sealing of marriage by the invocation of the blessing in order to bless and protect this release of the sacred fire.

LOVE BRINGS FORTH *a* CREATION

The true meaning of the ritual of sexual union in marriage is to exchange the sacred energies, express love, and balance the masculine and feminine polarities of the marriage partners. The light-energy resulting from this fusion enhances the positive qualities of each of the partners and strengthens their own divine identity, enabling them to carry and transmute their shared karma.

In the exchange of the sacred fire, our hearts overflow with love and we experience the very essence of the energies of creation. Each time the sexual union is practiced as a loving ritual between a husband and wife, a creation is brought forth. This may be a child, a work of art, or a service that you do together for humanity. Or it may be something less physical, perhaps an original idea, a feeling of joy, or an inspiration. Through the union of masculine and feminine energies, you are bringing forth something together that is greater than you can create separately. When you meditate on God during the marriage ritual, God will infuse your creation with a life that is transcending and ongoing.

The deeply personal connection between a husband and wife through sexual union also nourishes intimacy and attunement with each other. They share compassion and tenderness as well as gratitude and appreciation. When sexual union is spiritualized and in balance, a natural sense of buoyancy and vitality permeates the marriage relationship. Marriages can be more harmonious and happy because spiritual as well as emotional and physical needs are met. The couple can experience an expansiveness and creativity in their marriage. Such marriages are poised to offer greater service to their children, their communities, their professions, and the world.[2]

SEXUAL DESIRE

To love God in your husband or wife is the spiritualization of marriage. To adore and worship the light of God in your spouse is not disrespectful to God. Rather, it conveys the highest respect. It exalts the highest and the most noble in each other. It simply means that all of your energies, including sexual energies, can be spiritualized and you can experience love at the level of the divine union. You can love God in man or in woman and still experience physical attraction and sexual desire. How do you reconcile these feelings with the exalted experience?

Ultimately, sexual desire is the desire of God to bring forth the highest creativity in every aspect of life. It is the tremendous momentum of God desiring to be in physical manifestation, and it is the momentum of energy that is needed for the union of the seed and the egg. God did not create the universe without desire. He had to desire to have his universe. Likewise, in order for you to create, and this applies to any project or creation that you're undertaking, you must also have desire.

If you don't bring the fullness of your manhood or your womanhood into the momentum of desire, it's like a tiny little wave breaking on the shore because there is no desire behind it. Look at the marvelous bounding waves that are the big breakers and you understand the sense of desire you must have to build your life, to excel in a profession, to be an effective spouse or parent. You have to have so much desire that when the wave breaks on the shore of your life, it releases that much energy for creation.

When sexual desire is understood, the spiritualization of sex and procreation can become the natural experience of men and women. Instead of suppressing sexual desire, it is the translation of sexual desire into a divine creativity, and this change in consciousness can happen in the twinkling of an eye.

ORIGINAL SIN DOES NOT EXIST; YOUR ORIGIN IS *in* GOD

The doctrine of original sin, which is still taught today, states that as a result of the fall of Adam and Eve every member of the human race is born with a moral defect. Even though most of us reject this doctrine in our conscious mind, we may still harbor a sense of condemnation concerning sex at subconscious levels.

When I first learned about this doctrine as a child, I could not understand how the sins of someone who had lived five thousand or more years ago could make me a sinner. This teaching made no sense to me then and I don't believe it to this day.

Barely a trace of the concept of original sin can be found in the writings of the early apostolic fathers. It wasn't until the fifth century that the controversy over the doctrine of original sin erupted. Saint Augustine taught that the stain of original sin was transmitted from generation to generation by the sexual act itself. Because he thought that the sexual act was always accompanied by lust, he declared it inherently sinful.

Original sin does not exist, because our origin is in God. It is that simple. Thus, we can ask God to help us root out of our subconscious any lingering sense of impurity or condemnation about sex and procreation. We can be free from the prison house of guilt, shame, and confusion regarding sex.

SPIRITUALIZING *the* SEXUAL UNION

Without this guilt about sex and original sin, the joy of the sacred union can be restored. This sacred union mirrors the natural state of the soul's union with her Higher Self and with her God

Presence. In the marriage union of man and woman on earth, we approach the bliss of union with the Divine One.

The entire marriage ritual is an adoration to God. The love between the couple determines the purity and the light in the interchange of energies in the sacred union. This creative love guides all the actions that are shared in sexual union. It is not a mechanical process or a set of special techniques to bring out desired results. It is led by love. It is the welling up of love within you that brings everything else to pass in divine order.

This love is a communion you achieve by deep and heartfelt prayers and meditations to God before the marriage ritual. Through these prayers, you are drawing the light from the crown and the base-of-the-spine chakras into the heart in preparation for the descent and ascent of light. You bring this light to the heart by compassion and love for one another.

This meditation on the heart of one another is also for the purpose of expanding the fire of your heart and sending it to the heart of your spouse. This burning love within the heart brings forth sexual desire and union. It is not based primarily on the attraction of the senses nor the desire for a sensual experience, though there is a natural attraction between the wife and husband. The love of the heart brings forth the joy, the pleasure, and the spontaneity of sexual union.

The goal of your meditation is to be transported to the heights of spiritual attunement as you engage in the marriage ritual. To reach this level of attunement, you can select music, songs, decrees, prayers, or mantras that enable you to be spiritually uplifted and that honor your personal spiritual tradition and faith. Playing sacred music, including Christmas carols, is one of the best ways to permeate your home with a sense of holiness. It's important to choose your music carefully so that your energies are uplifted and not brought down through sensual lyrics or rhythms. You can also learn to discern the consciousness of those who are singing and choose recordings by people who have great love, angelic voices, or a deep devotion from the world's great spiritual traditions.

A period of silent meditation after sexual union to complete the raising and sealing of the energies in the third-eye chakra enhances spiritual fulfillment so that excess energies are not left in the lower chakras. The third-eye chakra can act as a magnet to raise the energies of your body. This is the renewal action that uplifts and inspires one another. How wonderful God is that he has given us this experience and that he can be so near in the love we share!

The greatest secret of life, the secret of creation, is sacred. You can think of your consciousness as an arrow that you shoot high into the cosmos in the moment of uniting with God in one another during sexual union. And the aim of the arrow, of your consciousness, is the thrust of your love and your desire. It is God's desire within you to see your arrow reach the highest star—the soul of your child-to-be or another beautiful creation of love.

High in the Himalayas of India, the following couple experienced the arrow of their love reaching to the very soul of their child-to-be.

> *A few years before I met my East Indian husband, he had a vision, while up in the Himalayas, of a soul who wanted to be born to him one day. After three years of marriage and preparation to become parents, we journeyed to the source of the Ganges in the Himalayas, a place far removed from civilization that took many days to travel to, both driving and on foot.*
>
> *Once there, each one of us spent an entire day by ourselves—my husband doing his own special meditations and I doing mine, accompanied by violet flame and other prayers to purify ourselves and transmute past karma that might need to be cleared before we conceived a child. I prayed for the protection of the holy conception and gestation of this soul. When we came together that night, we were in a reverent state of mind and very quiet, envi-*

sioning the union of the divine masculine and the divine feminine, the energies of Shiva and Shakti, as they are known in the Eastern tradition, comingling and ascending.

This was over twenty years ago, and now that same child, our daughter, has made her way back to the Himalayas on a special journey, where she is working on a project as a journalist. It is truly amazing to see how this has come full circle and how her soul has been brought back to her spiritual home once again, through a tremendous opportunity that God opened up for her in miraculous ways.

THE CIRCLE *of* ONENESS

The circle of oneness is a ritual you can use to consecrate your sacred union and to seal the marriage ritual in the purity of God's love. You can also use this ritual to celebrate your oneness with your twin flame and with God. It is symbolic of the circle of the divine whole, or tai chi. Within the circle, you feel the fusion of the Father-Mother God, of love being fulfilled in love. You can also consecrate your love to your soul's reunion with your God Presence and to the ultimate reunion of you and your twin flame within the hallowed circle of God.

Begin by meditating upon the flame of love that burns within your heart. Visualize the arc of your love ascending from your heart to the heart of your God Presence. Take your right hand and dip it into the fires of your heart and draw a circle of white light around you and your spouse. Visualize this circle of light, twelve feet in diameter, as a line of sacred fire and see yourselves within this protected circle of oneness.

Then give the following prayer for you and your spouse in order to protect and seal the exchange of sacred energies. You can also pray for the angels of love and the holy cherubim to protect your marriage union.

In the name of God and in the name of Higher Selves, we call to you, beloved angels of love, to draw the circle of your oneness around us as we stand in adoration of the one true God. Make this sacred circle of oneness twelve feet in diameter, a line of sacred fire, a ring-pass-not against all that would oppose our loving union.

Let our love be consecrated for our soul's ultimate reunion with our God.

We invoke the covering cherubim to guard our love in the planes of matter this day and to help us manifest the honor, patience, and tenderness of divine love in our union. We accept this done right now in full power.

MANTRAS *and* MEDITATIONS *for* SACRED UNION

The following mantra is an affirmation that you and your spouse can give together to affirm your oneness with the Father-Mother God—with God as Father and Mother within you. The Father-Mother God is the center of all life. All life springs forth from this perfect union—the union of the Father in Spirit and the Mother in matter, the essential masculine and feminine polarity of creation.

I and my Father are one.
I and my Mother are one.

A great support for married couples is the loving presence of the Divine Mother, East and West—Kuan Yin, the Eastern bodhisattva, and Mary, the mother of Jesus. These representatives of God as Mother can assist you in any area of your life, including your relationships, marriage, and family. Giving their mantras can bring spiritual light into your marriage ritual.

Kuan Yin is the Mother of Mercy, the saviouress whose beauty, grace, and compassion is revered in temples, homes, and wayside grottoes throughout the Orient. (See Plate 7.) She is also honored among a growing number of devotees in the West. Kuan Yin is often portrayed with a child in her arms, near her feet or on her knees, or with several children around her. Her merciful heart brings succor and guidance to souls in need. The name Kuan Shih Yin, as she is often called, means literally "the one who regards, looks on, or hears the sounds of the world." According to legend, Kuan Yin was about to enter heaven but paused on the threshold as the cries of the world reached her ears. Many believe that she will respond to the simple recitation of her name.

Mary, the mother of Jesus, is traditionally regarded as the Queen of Angels. (See Plate 8.) She is very close to the people of earth, as evidenced by her many appearances around the globe. Although she has been traditionally revered by Catholics, we can all claim her as our mother, our sister, our teacher, and our friend.

We send our devotion to Mary by giving the Hail Mary prayer. When we say "Hail Mary," it means "Hail, Ma-ray," or "Hail Mother ray." Each time we say this prayer, we are giving salutation to the Mother light within us and within all life. This activates the light of the kundalini, and it slowly rises. When you offer this prayer to Mary, she can transfer her light to you for holding the vision of the highest good for you and your spouse.

The words of this Hail Mary differ slightly from the traditional version, which affirms that we are sinners. God does not want us to see ourselves as sinners. Rather, we can affirm our identity as sons and daughters of God and ask Mary to pray for our victory over sin, disease, and death.

You can also ask Mary to place her immaculate heart over your heart to help solve any problems in your life. Many people believe they have experienced healing through her intercession. No problem is too great or small for her attention.

To help spiritualize the sexual union and to receive the blessings and intercessions of these two Divine Mothers into your life, you can meditate on their images and give the following mantras as many times as you like.

MANTRAS TO KUAN YIN

Om Mani Padme Hum
(Hail to the jewel in the lotus)

Hail, greatly merciful Kuan Shih Yin!

PRAYER TO MARY

Hail, Mary, full of grace!
The Lord is with thee.
Blessed art thou among women
And blessed is the fruit of thy womb, Jesus.
Holy Mary, Mother of God,
Pray for us, sons and daughters of God,
Now and at the hour of our victory
Over sin, disease and death.

There is no greater comfort in the universe than to know that you are a soul loved by the Father-Mother God. As you receive this love and comfort in your heart, you can impart it as the greatest gift to your marriage, your family, and beyond.

QUESTIONS & ANSWERS

with Elizabeth Clare Prophet on

Marriage and the Spiritual Path

GETTING READY *to* TAKE *the* LEAP!

Q: When I want to get married, what should I look for? Should I look for a soul mate or a twin flame?

A: When you're looking to get married, you should forget about all of this. You should look to be in love. You should look to have the greatest devotion to this person that you could ever conceive of and the greatest desire to spend the rest of your life loving him.

Why try to put a label on love. You can pray to God. You can ask if this is right and you can call for guidance. But honestly and truly, what is real is how you feel and how you love. And we grow in our sense of love. Possessive loves are possessive loves; they're very limiting. Then there are deeper loves and spiritual loves. The higher we go in our own evolution, the more we perceive what kind of love we are seeking.

When you read about people who have been through a divorce, they often say that they finally woke up one day and realized that they've been attracting the same type of person over and over again. For instance, perhaps they've been attracted to someone they had to take care of or they felt sorry for. Well, at the time that they married, that was their definition of love. Then they realized that sympathy is not a good foundation for marriage. You've got to have more than sympathy. Feeling sorry for people won't be a benefit for you or them.

For many of us, if we don't overcome certain things in our psychology, we will attract the identical kind of person that we may have just broken up with or divorced—the same problems, the same personality but in a different body. This pattern might continue until we can see through our own vulnerabilities and come to a higher place. That's the danger of jumping into a new relationship or remarrying too quickly. People may not have changed enough to marry someone who is at a higher level because they themselves haven't gotten to a higher level.

So, you see, eventually we can understand and perceive what is attracting us to a certain kind of relationship. Then we can decide if we want to maintain a relationship on that level or if we want something more. If you realize that you do want something more, then you can adjust what you're looking for.

Q: **How will I know when I'm whole enough to commit to marriage? I've been in the same relationship for the past two years and it's developing quite nicely.**

A: Well, one of the reasons we get married is that while we're striving for wholeness it's helpful to have someone who complements us. It's a matter of knowing the areas where we lack wholeness, whether or not we can live with ourself in that state and whether our mate can live with us as well. It's also a question of knowing the areas of incompleteness in our mate but being able to say, "I love this person enough to make up the difference, to supply the other side in the relationship." And one is very happy to give one's strengths in return for the gift of another's strengths, and that is like the symbol of the tai chi in the divine whole.

To some degree each one fills in the gap of the incompleteness in the other. However, that doesn't mean that one supplies the wholeness for another that each one must supply for himself. The problem is when you don't recognize your absence of wholeness, so you may expect the other person to be everything, to fill in those parts of yourself that only you can fill in. Maturity is going into a marriage without expecting that your mate is going to supply the things that you ought to be finding in God, in your heart, and in your own Higher Self.

There is a relationship with God that no one else can replace, no one else can fulfill. And if you try to make someone you're married to, even your twin flame, fulfill that relationship, you will always be disappointed. There is a place in your being that is only for you and God, and that is something you also need to know. You have to be able to retreat to that place when you experience the ups and downs of life.

Rather than thinking in terms of wholeness, you need to see if you are mature enough to say, "I can deal with the marriage. I can deal with my karma and his karma. I can deal with the eventualities, whatever they may be, because our love, and our love for God, is greater than all these things."

Q: How can I prepare for marriage so that problems are minimal?

A: If you are supposed to marry in this life, you can pray for the protection of the person you are supposed to be married to, even if you've never seen that person. Other important ways to prepare yourself include pursuing psychological and physical healing, serving others and serving God, and bettering yourself.

You may not be ready yet for the person you're going to marry. I often think that two people who are supposed to meet are like two stars in the heavens and each one of them is on a trajectory moving through cosmos. Only when they reach the point where their paths cross can they find one another. They will not reach that point unless both of them are on an upward spiral, moving forward and not satisfied to be today what they were yesterday. But they are continually looking at the bright new day as an opportunity to unfold more of themselves.

You don't want to marry someone if that person is content with the way he is, has no desire to go beyond it, and wants to add you to his life because he thinks you will complement him nicely and enable him to stay at the plateau he has reached. And you have to know and observe people to see if they are striving, because if you are a mover, you will not only cross paths with them but you will go far beyond them. So part of your preparation may be to determine if your partner is moving forward in life to the same degree that you are, and vice versa. This is an important deciding factor in how far your relationship can go.

Q: **What can we do to help our marriage when we are not on the same spiritual path? And what can I do about my husband being discordant?**

A: First of all, you and your spouse don't necessarily have to be on the same spiritual path. But whatever the situation is, the main thing you can do is to pray for loved ones rather than struggle with them. Hold a positive vision of their potential and who they really are. Be the servant. Don't be afraid to serve your husband or your wife. It's not degrading. It doesn't show inequality; it shows love. We can serve and wait on our husband or wife without feeling that we have in any way compromised our selfhood.

To continue to love and to give love is the most you can do for a husband or wife whom you feel is discordant. To call for the violet flame to transmute those energies is also helpful. You can pray to the angels, including Archangel Michael. Pray for his protection.

Don't give up just because you may be having a few problems in your home. Give it a good try, infusing the situation with light and prayer. And increase your level of sacrifice, increase your level of surrender.

What are you going to put into the marriage? You are going

to get out everything you put into it. You are going to reap the rewards of joy. Put more into it and don't be self-righteous and don't be justifying yourself when you think you've been wronged. That's a trap. Just give, give more.

The other person will become more beautiful, more wonderful through that process. Or if he is not the right person, he may become worse because he cannot stand the purity of your love.

So your love towards an individual will bring out the greatest and the worst. And when the worst parts come out, we have the utmost compassion. And that compassion may need to be extended seventy times seven, forgiving until God tells us, "This person is not going to change. It's time for you to move on."

AFFAIRS *and* DIVORCE

Q: **Why are extramarital affairs so common? I feel like I'm too young to get married, but when I do, I don't want this to happen.**

A: There are many reasons for affairs. People sometimes have affairs to experiment or to act out fantasies. They may be trying to compensate for unfulfilled romances or boring marriages. Some may be thrill seekers. Others may come from families where infidelity occurred, and they are therefore reenacting the situations that they witnessed in their formative years.

In addition, affairs can occur in relationships where people are working with each other for an immediate and common purpose and spending long hours together. This is common given the expectations of our modern culture or when people don't have a commitment to their marriage. These affairs may last for a few months, six months, a year, or longer, and all of a sudden they're over. And so a person can go through many affairs, for instance, over a fifty-year span of living and working. And unfortunately, this is not uncommon in our society.

When the affairs are over, the life force is spent. People don't have a net gain from having gone through these relationships, because affairs are not lawful. What they should have gained from the positive project in each relationship has become the spending of energy.

Another situation is that sometimes when a couple decides to be celibate, they may then develop attractions to others. Although they may sincerely intend to abstain from sexual relations, they may not actually have the mastery of their sexual energies that they need in order to stay celibate. Celibacy then becomes a forced spirituality beyond their level of attainment. So while people are trying to remain celibate in their marriage, they become attracted to people outside the marriage.

Whatever the nature of the affair, it is an opposition to the sacred love of the marriage union and, as we know, it can destroy that union.

Q: If we've struggled for years in our marriage but we're still not resolved about everything, should we get a divorce?

A: Well, it may or may not be time for a divorce. I believe in working, and working hard, at a marriage. We ought to try to make our marriages succeed. And I believe that we should always be giving love, beyond the person of our spouse, to God. Our devotion is to God and to our twin flame.

But if it absolutely doesn't work, then we ought to be smart enough to recognize it, pray about it, and see to it that we don't overstay our lawful time in the relationship. We don't want to create more karma and waste both partners' lives when we could be accomplishing more good without the burden of a relationship that is obviously leading neither party in any constructive direction.

Spouses should search their own souls to discover whether or not they have done all in their power to bring harmony to a marriage and a home and to make a go of it. If there is so much disagreement and discord that it is more costly to the partners to remain together than it would be to separate, then it may be in their best interest to go their separate ways. Of course every couple's situation is different, but love must be the dominant theme. You should never leave anyone, especially in this kind of relationship, except in the purest of love, forgiveness, and understanding. If you are going to part, you should strive to let go of all bitterness and go your way in peace.

KEYS *to a* SUCCESSFUL MARRIAGE

Q: **Can you give me guidelines on how a married couple can work together to make practical decisions?**

A: In every relationship, whether it's between friends or marriage partners, there are decisions that don't matter: What shall we eat? Where shall we go? What shall we wear? What time shall we do this?

Then there are more important matters: How are we going to spend our money? How many children are we going to have? Where are we going to live?

There are a lot of decisions that affect both partners. And if you come to an impasse, remember what Mark always taught: You don't have to make up your mind on the instant.

If you perceive that there is something not quite right in your spouse's perceptions or he lacks an awareness of a larger picture that would influence the decision in a different way, you can pray to your spouse's Higher Self and to God for the right understanding and resolution. Be gracious enough to allow him to go through the process of arriving at the right conclusion, because nobody is perfect and nobody can arrive at these decisions all at once.

If you have a confrontation and you're insisting on your way, both ways may be wrong. So you may want to find a way to postpone the decision by taking a break or gathering more information to get a fuller perspective.

In our personal lives, we've all known that we ourselves can feel very strongly about something because we know, for instance, five facts about a situation. And therefore, we're all for going this way, we're all for this political candidate, we're all for doing a certain thing. And two weeks later we learn five more facts and we're turned around to another way of looking at things.

When everything is in view and you've prayed for inner guidance, then it's easier to lean upon the other person and say okay. And when that decision is in agreement with your Higher Self, then you're at peace. But if someone in your life makes a decision for you and it doesn't feel right inside, you need to figure out a harmonious way to resolve the situation and to trust God to help you work through it.

Mark often said to us, "Trust no man." We cannot trust one another's human self. We have to trust God to use that person as an instrument for his will and his decision. It's an important lesson to understand. Otherwise, you'll become idolaters of your husband or your wife and you'll say, "Okay, this person can do no wrong." And then you're abdicating your own inner wisdom and self-respect.

Q: **What is the biggest piece of advice you can give on making my marriage last for the long haul?**

A: Don't nag. That's my advice. When the wife nags the husband, picking at this and picking at that, it emasculates the man. It eats at him and keeps him from being the strength he is intended to be in the marriage and in the home. Being nagged at constantly is one of the worst things for a person to live with, and it just ruins the relationship. Whether it is the man nagging the woman or the woman nagging the man, it's the same thing. It shouldn't happen in a loving relationship.

Another thing is, don't try to change him. If you don't like the way he is, don't marry him. This is one of the biggest mistakes people make. I've seen couples who have gotten married, the wife thinking that once they're married she'll get the husband to stop drinking, stop gambling, stop smoking, or whatever the case may be, and it just doesn't work.

Q: **Can two strong and independent people who are pursuing personal careers have a good marriage?**

A: You certainly can have a career and fulfill your desire for motherhood and childbearing. You both need to figure out where in the cycle of the unfoldment of your marriage each of these things is going to appear and in what order, whether simultaneously or in succession. If God has a mission for you together, then you must know that he also has a plan whereby each of your talents can be fulfilled in harmony.

So you look at the priorities of those things which you can only accomplish together and then those things which each of you need to accomplish individually. Along with this, you can invoke the violet flame to remove the rough places in your relationship.

If the relationship is worthwhile, then it's worth being committed to. If the love is there, then love by nature is self-sacrificing for both people, especially for two strong individuals.

And so it's unfortunate that when people have careers and strong personalities, they think that because of that the relationship won't work. And really that's why it should work, because people do need to feel within their mate the same strength that they have in themselves and to be able to admire it and work with it.

You wouldn't be happy if you weren't with a powerful person and he wouldn't have fulfillment if you weren't powerful either. So you can dedicate yourselves to one another and your mission and believe in the fact that it can work if you make it work. And you both have the benefit of being with someone whom you can respect and work things out with, because your spouse has a strength that matches your own.

PLANNING *a* FAMILY

Q: **What about family planning and birth control?**

A: Parents should not bring forth more children than they are able to care for or more children than they are able to love. It is right to plan your family and to plan it in the best way you know how. If you decide you don't want more children, then it's proper to pursue some method of birth control.

Whatever this method is, it's advisable for it to be the least harmful to the mother, such as barrier methods, and for it to not be permanent, because your circumstances may change.

Unless there is jeopardy to the life of the mother, abortion as a means of birth control is considered a violation of the sacred flame of life. Therefore other means of predetermining the family circle should be studied and applied. For when life, sacred life, is at stake, one does not act haphazardly as though the choice to bear children is a decision after conception has occurred. God as a living potential is in the child from the moment of conception.

Q: **What if I had a vasectomy and now want a child?**

A: If the type of operation is not permanent, try to have it undone. If it is permanent, then consider whether you should adopt a child. Adoption is also an important option for couples to consider. Realize that God can bring you the same soul through adoption that you may have had through normal conception.

You can also consider whether you might wish to sponsor life by being a teacher or helping incoming souls in some other way.

Q: **What if I'm married but don't have a desire for children?**

A: You and your spouse must feel the calling from your heart to have children and to bear the responsibility to love, care for, and educate them. Some couples choose not to have children and this is of course perfectly fine. Their gift to life may be another kind of offering that is unique to them. The couple may offer a service together or separately but, in any case, the love that the couple shares becomes the foundation for whatever service they choose as their gift to life.

THE GIFT *of* MARRIAGE

Q: How can I know if my marriage is based on human emotions or a deep spiritual connection? I've played music with a lot of other people, and I've never experienced anything like when I play music with my wife. As musicians, we know that music stirs up a lot of emotions. And one is never quite sure if the emotion is just a human feeling or if it's something that is divine.

A: Love is something like the bird that we want to capture and keep in our hearts. We don't like the ephemeral nature of love in any form. I have found that when people are searching for these answers in life, they don't always know what the answer is when they are close to a situation. But as they continue their own interior growth, they begin to have a greater perspective, a co-measurement of their own interior light, measuring, then, the experiences they have had in their life. I myself am far more capable today of evaluating experiences I've had than I was at the time I had them.

And we would like to hope that what we are experiencing is of the highest, that it is everlasting and profound, especially in matters of the interchange in relationships. It is human nature to seek the permanence of love.

When we love, we love deeply. We love our friends, we love people we meet. And when we clearly perceive that that which comes back to us is not the profound love we thought it was, it can be one of life's deepest disappointments. It's a great disappointment to experience the loss of faith in a friend, an acquaintance or a business partner, the sense of someone not being faithful to an ideal, to a purpose of any kind.

Just trust the decisions you have made, the harmony you have kept, the fact that the marriage is fruitful and blessed, and that you continue to have these experiences and they continue to mount.

You don't seem to have a real index that is giving you the opposite evidence about your relationship. You're not receiving warnings. Sometimes God reveals them to us as intimations that are almost subconscious, and they surface very quickly and then they leave. They challenge our conception about ourselves at that moment, and so we don't want to admit, perhaps, what others may see very clearly. But we don't want to admit it because at our present level of development, this is where we have positioned ourselves. This is where we have decided to plant the flame of our love, and we want it to work. We're working out a karma, we're working out a situation.

So if I were you in the situation of your marriage, I would trust what is self-evident—that you have this unique experience because it is divine, because you have an inner union.

I think that you have this special experience with her rather than with any other musician because there is obviously the divine cause behind the relationship and a good resonance of souls. It's like a soul harmony that you have. There is a harmony that's very deep between you on which the cosmos can resonate when you play. It's an affinity. You probably would never have married if you had not had a profound revelation that there was a great calling, an inner knowing, and a past awareness of one another.

It's important not to pick apart the petals of the flower, not to uproot the rose bush. Let things be as they are and enjoy them for what they are.

It's very wonderful that you are happy. You need to protect that happiness and protect that bliss. It's fine to ask this question about it, but then you can let go of the sense of questioning. It's a beautiful gift, so you can accept it for what it is. Give all of your love to it and pray for its protection.

It's like the alchemy of God. You think of the most perfect alchemy you can conceive of and you give it to God. And he reviews it, purifies it, and gives it back to you with corrections. It's like a teacher grading a paper. So he will show you how it can be even better and more beautiful.

God loves us when we're satisfied in life in that we accept little gifts and great gifts. We all have many gifts in our lives, great and small. And without demanding perfection from anyone, we can love and be loved and perceive love, and we know that God is there just behind the veil.

NOTES

PART ONE · TWIN FLAMES AND SOUL MATES

Chapter 2: Twin Flames

1. Based on Barry Vissell and Joyce Vissell's book *The Shared Heart: Relationship Initiations and Celebrations* (Aptos, Calif.: Ramira Publishing, 1984), pp. 30–31; and "Moses Mendelssohn," at NNDB, accessed April 29, 2015, http://www.nndb.com/people/141 /000093859/.
2. Matt. 19:6; Mark 10:9.
3. Isa. 54:5.
4. *Winston and Clementine: The Personal Letters of the Churchills*, ed. Mary Soames (New York: Houghton Mifflin, 1999), p. 38.

Chapter 3: Soul Mates

1. "Stories of Famous Lovers," "Abigail and John Adams," accessed April 2, 2015, http://www.bonzasheila.com/stories/abigailjohnadams .html.
2. "Abigail Adams Biography," Encyclopedia of World Biography, accessed April 2, 2015, http://www.notablebiographies.com/A-An /Adams-Abigail.html.
3. Edith B. Gelles, *Abigail and John: Portrait of a Marriage* (New York: Harper Perennial, 2010), p. x.
4. Ibid, p 284.

PART TWO · KARMA AND RELATIONSHIPS

Chapter 4: Karmic Relationships

1. Similar aspects of our psychology absorbed from parents and others have also been described as the inner masculine and inner feminine. For more information, see *The Invisible Partners: How the Male and*

Female in Each of Us Affects Our Relationships, by John A. Sanford (Mahwah, N.J.: Paulist Press, 1980); *Sacred Psychology of Love: The Quest for Relationships That Unite Heart and Soul,* by Marilyn C. Barrick, Ph.D. (Gardiner, Mont.: Summit University Press, 1999); and *Getting the Love You Want: A Guide for Couples,* by Harville Hendrix, Ph.D. (New York: Owl Books, Henry Holt, 1988).

2. For more on healing the inner child, see *Healing Your Aloneness: Finding Love and Wholeness through Your Inner Child,* by Erika J. Chopich and Margaret Paul (New York: HarperCollins, 1990); *Inner Bonding: Becoming a Loving Adult to Your Inner Child,* by Margaret Paul, Ph.D. (Harper San Francisco, 1990); and *The Inner Child Workbook: What to Do with Your Past When It Just Won't Go Away,* by Cathryn L. Taylor (New York: Jeremy P. Tarcher/Putnam, 1991). Other resources for healing your psychology include *8 Keys to Building Your Best Relationships,* by Daniel Hughes (New York: W.W. Norton & Co, 2013), and *Getting Past Your Past: Take Control of Your Life with Self-Help Techniques from EMDR Therapy,* by Francine Shapiro (New York: Rodale, Inc., 2013).

For healing the inner child, Mrs. Prophet encouraged the study and application of the teachings of Dr. Maria Montessori, who developed an inspired teaching method to unlock the potential of the child. For online Montessori parent and teacher training and resources, see http://www.ageofmontessori.org.

3. Kahlil Gibran, *The Prophet* (1923; reprint, New York: Alfred A. Knopf, 1960), pp. 58–59.

Chapter 5: Healing and Transforming Relationships

1. Because of its vibratory action and proximity to earthly substance, the violet light can combine with any molecule or molecular structure, any particle of matter known or unknown, and any wave of light, electrons, or electricity. When we invoke the violet flame, it envelops each atom individually. Instantaneously a polarity is set up between the nucleus of the atom and the white light in the core of the flame. The nucleus, being matter, assumes the negative pole. And the light of the violet flame, being Spirit, assumes the positive pole.

The interaction between the nucleus of the atom and the light in the violet flame establishes an oscillation. This oscillation dislodges the misqualified energies from the past that are trapped between the electrons orbiting the nucleus. As this substance is loosened, the electrons begin to move more freely and the debris is thrown into the violet flame.

This action takes place at nonphysical, or metaphysical, dimensions of matter. On contact with the violet flame, the dense substance is transmuted, restored to its native purity and returned to one's Higher Self. It may take repeated work with the violet flame to completely transmute this substance.

2. For more teaching on the violet flame, see *Violet Flame to Heal Body, Mind and Soul,* by Elizabeth Clare Prophet (Gardiner, Mont.: Summit University Press, 1997).

PART THREE · SEXUALITY AND SPIRITUALITY

Chapter 6: Sex and Energy Flow

1. For more information on the chakras, see *Your Seven Energy Centers,* by Elizabeth Clare Prophet (Gardiner, Mont.: Summit University Press, 2000).

Chapter 7: Sexual Relationships and Practices

1. For more information on the negative impact of casual sex, see *The End of Sex: How Hookup Culture Is Leaving a Generation Unhappy, Sexually Unfulfilled, and Confused About Intimacy,* by Donna Freitas (New York: Basic Books, 2013), and *Reviving Ophelia: Saving the Selves of Adolescent Girls,* by Mary Pipher, Ph.D. (New York: Riverhead Books, 2005).

PART FOUR · MARRIAGE AND THE SPIRITUAL PATH

Chapter 9: Marriage: A Soul Perspective

1. For more on marriage, see *Heart Centered Marriage: Fulfilling Our Natural Desire for Sacred Partnership,* by Sue Patton Thoele (n.p.: Conari Press, 1996); *Conscious Loving: The Journey to Co- Commitment,* by Gay Hendricks, Ph.D., and Kathlyn Hendricks, Ph.D. (New York: Bantam Books, 1990); and *Saving Your Marriage Before It Starts: Seven Questions to Ask Before—and After—You Marry,* exp. and updated ed., by Drs. Les and Leslie Parrott (Grand Rapids, Mich.: Zondervan, 2006).

Chapter 10: The Marriage Ritual

1. Gen. 1:3.

2. For additional teachings on the marriage ritual for conception, meditations for pregnancy, and parenting, see *Nurturing Your Baby's Soul: A Spiritual Guide for Expectant Parents,* by Elizabeth Clare Prophet (Gardiner, Mont.: Summit University Press, 1998) and *Family Designs for the Golden Age* and *Freedom of the Child,* by Elizabeth Clare Prophet, on MP3 CD; available from the bookstore at www.SummitLighthouse.org.

SUMMIT UNIVERSITY ☙ PRESS®

RELATED TITLES

Soul Mates and Twin Flames
Alchemy of the Heart
The Creative Power of Sound
Violet Flame to Heal Body, Mind and Soul
The Story of Your Soul
Access the Power of Your Higher Self
Your Seven Energy Centers
Karma and Reincarnation

OTHER TITLES

The Art of Practical Spirituality
Odyssey of Your Soul
Talk with Angels

Gardens of the Heart gift book series:
Compassion, Forgiveness, Joy, Gratitude,
Love, Hope, Peace and Kindness

SUMMIT UNIVERSITY ☙ PRESS ESPAÑOL™

LIBROS

En busca del amor ideal (primavera 2016)
Almas compañeras y llamas gemelas (otoño 2015)
Tus siete centros de energía (otoño 2015)
La odisea de tu alma
Conversaciones con los ángeles
La serie Jardines del corazón
(Compasión, Perdón, Alegría, Gratitud,
Amor, Esperanza, Bondad y Paz)

ALCHEMY OF THE HEART
How to Give and Receive More Love
by Elizabeth Clare Prophet

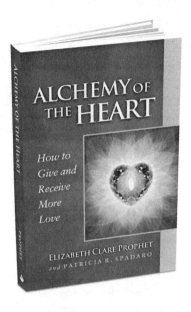

These sensitive, profound and rare insights help us gain entrée into the most precious, and misunderstood, component of our being—the heart. They show us that while love can be compassionate and nurturing, it can also be powerful, dynamic and practical—a catalyst for spiritual growth.

You'll learn how the mature heart overcomes hidden blocks to giving and receiving more love. How you can soften and strengthen the heart to create more meaningful relationships in all areas of your life. And how even the most intense lessons of love, if we are willing to learn from them, can be the open door to a higher way of loving.

ISBN 978-0-922729-60-9   204 PAGES $8.95

SUMMIT UNIVERSITY ꙮ PRESS®

VIOLET FLAME
TO HEAL BODY, MIND AND SOUL
by Elizabeth Clare Prophet

Learn how to use the violet flame, a high-frequency spiritual energy, to increase vitality, overcome blocks to healing and create positive change in your personal life and for the planet. Discover how the violet flame can be used to assist any healing process of the body, mind, emotions or spirit.

Includes inspiring true stories and nine easy steps to begin using the violet flame with affirmations, mantras, and visualizations.

ISBN 978-0-922729-37-1   108 PAGES $8.95

SUMMIT UNIVERSITY 🕯 PRESS®

YOUR SEVEN ENERGY CENTERS

A Holistic Approach to
Physical, Emotional and Spiritual Vitality
by Elizabeth Clare Prophet

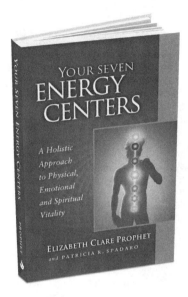

Your Seven Energy Centers contains powerful insights and tools for wholeness based on the science of the body's subtle energy system. It draws from the wisdom of the world's spiritual traditions to show how you can nurture your soul through seven stages of personal growth.

Includes an overview of holistic techniques that help restore the body's energetic balance—from homeopathy, vitamins and spa therapies to meditation, affirmation and visualization.

> *"Marries ancient healing wisdom with practical spiritual insights to help you create your own dynamic and uniquely personal healing journey. Your 21st-century guide to integrating and healing body, mind and soul."* —ANN LOUISE GITTLEMAN
> author of *The Living Beauty Detox Program*

ISBN 978-0-922729-56-2   234 PAGES $8.95

SUMMIT UNIVERSITY 🕭 PRESS®